It's No Secret

Thriving After Surviving

Danielle Downey

ISBN: 978-1730823060
ISBN-13

Table of Contents

Preface:

I always wanted to be a gymnast. But, without training it was tough. It was said that I spent more time on my hands walking than I did on my feet, but that wasn't meant to be my future.

Then I aspired to be a writer. I mean, I have always written as a form of release, from around the age of six whether that's poetry or stories, yet I never believed that anyone may want to read them. So, they stayed a secret, like so much of my past.

The writing was a good secret, a little bit of me that I owned and was in control of, in an environment where I often felt that I had little control of my own body and mind.
A far cry from the dirty, putrid and revolting secret like the abuse that was perpetrated towards me by people who should have loved me that I carried around on my shoulders for so many, many years.

That was until July 2017 when I decided that the time had come to share my true story with the world. To share my story of a little girl brought up in a home riddled with violence, neglect, incest and isolation. Who knew she was different in so many ways to her friends and felt totally unworthy of the love and commitment that all children deserve. Who knew that she had so much that she wanted to do and could fulfil, given half the chance.

And so, this is MY story. Written from my memories, perceptions and recollections. Some hazy and wonderful and some vibrant, bright yet deeply distressing.

This is the story of a little girl who refused to give in. To lie down and be broken just because she happened to be born into a gene pool that was not of her choosing and who felt those emotions that may survivors may have felt of loneliness, danger and hopelessness. To want love but be unable to ask for it. To want kindness and fairness but be unable to articulate it and to feel so broken that you feel like a spare part in the freakish jigsaw of your life.

This was me. Before I began my road from surviving to thriving. Before I was able to take from the trauma of my life the lessons I had learned, the resilience I had built up and the huge amount of inner strength that I could manifest once I stopped believing that I was the root of all of my problems and grew to love and appreciate myself and all that I am.

I have never asked for sympathy, nor for you to understand me, but what I do ask is that you take this book as it is intended. As a reality check that we have within us greatness. A greatness to succeed and survive no matter what carnage and upset, trials and tribulations, challenges and adversities are lying before us. And realise that you, like me can decide to thrive and live your best life, is a way designed and articulated by you, and only you.

I have tried to recreate events to the best of my ability and as truthfully as possible from my memories of them. The conversations and events are not written to represent word for word transcripts. Rather, I have recalled them as best I could in a way that evokes the meaning of what was said.

Names and situations have been changed within the context of the book to protect the innocent as per the laws of our land. Many of those ironically are not that innocent in my eyes.

But because this book is not their story, but mine, told through my memories and from my perspective I am ok with that. This then, is my story, It's No Secret, Thriving after Surviving.

Acknowledgements

I have been supported through my journey by so many inspiring and fantastic people, without whom I would never have got It's No Secret into print.

To Sharon Bott and Melanie Pledger for showing me my full potential, believing in me and enabling me to find the courage to begin to write after partaking in the DNA Light Up programme.

To Abigail Horne, Sarah Stone and all of the team at Author's and Co. for their help, guidance and input in getting this into print. For your patience, kindness and knowledge, I thank you.

To Helene and Cathy for their press shots and book cover shoot. You made me feel and look amazing and I thank you too.

To the support services who offered me counselling and support when I was well and truly broken, thank you. Your commitment to supporting and empowering survivors on increasingly smaller budgets is magnificent and I for one would not be where I am today without your input.

To my wonderful husband Charlie. My rock, my friend, my soul mate. Without you by my side every step of the way for the last fifteen years I would never have got to learn to love and trust. Your love makes me whole, complete and I am a better person for having you in my life.

For my six beautiful children, all different, all marvelous. I love you with every breath in my body with every heartbeat to the moon and back again and so much more than chocolate cake!

To the amazing people I have met, friends I have made and people who I have learned so much from on my journey I thank you all too. For being by my side, for loving and sharing my life, the chaos and the wonder and for believing in me when I often did not believe in me one bit.

If you would have told me four years ago that I would be stronger, happier and more focused than ever having written my first book I would have laughed openly at you, yet here it is! A doorway for others to step through to begin their journey and the beginning of the next stage of my journey as a writer and speaker.

I seek now to enable others to heal, share their stories and live their lives as they design while I bang the drum on their behalf, breaking the silences and shouting loudly and proudly that I am a survivor, no longer defined by my past and that they too can live their best life. In sharing our stories, we take the power away from abusers and bring sexual violence to the forefront so that it is not treated like a dirty, shameful secret.

To those who have taken the time to connect with me already and bravely shared their stories with me, their dream's and hopes I salute you all. We are stronger than we think, and I stand beside you all, waving you on into your brighter and more colourful futures.

Please do connect with me on social media @crazykids48 or Danielledowney.co.uk

Chapter 1 Alone

As the pushchair bumped clumsily up the kerb I woke up. Pushchairs in 1976 had no suspension, just fabric seats and little comfort. It was dark and cold, and the streetlights were bright in the night sky where the stars twinkled above.

I squinted my eyes half shut and was fascinated by the way the lamp light extended wider and thinner as my eyes narrowed. I was in my pyjamas and knew that I had been asleep in my warm bed with its cheerful Paddington Bear duvet cover. I did not know where we were going as my dad bumped the buggy up and down the pavements, and I would guess that I was around three years of age.

That night I was left to sleep on a floor in an unfamiliar room. It was cold I recall. I didn't know where my dad was, and no one came when I cried out in the dark. The unfamiliarity of the room with the closed door made me feel abandoned. I had no concept of time, but I was aware that the light at some point came through the crack in the curtains.

It was lonely in that room and I was afraid. I do not remember the front of the house or what came before those memories, nor going home after the cold dark night, which I think are my earliest recollections of my life. The bewilderment and terror of being abandoned are feelings that I identified with for many, many years.

I know that me and my dad went to that house many times so that my dad could see his girlfriend. She was a single mum to two boys, all whom remain faceless. I am glad that I can't remember what they looked like because of what was to come. It makes the atrocities easier to file away.

What I do remember is that my dad was around twenty-three years old at this point in time and liked the ladies. I have been told that he was a good-looking young man, before he turned into a bitter and twisted human being inside and out. He was short in stature and had large almond eyes and long lashes, both of which I have inherited. I don't remember going to the house again late at night, but I do realise that we went back multiple times.

I wonder if I made so much noise whilst shut in the room, that I put paid to the activities which were going on. So, with the overnight escapades ceased we began to go back in the day time, or early evening. It was during these forays, while my father was entertaining himself, I was left alone at the mercy of the two faceless, nameless boys.

I was encouraged to play in their bedrooms with them for hours. I didn't particularly like boy's toys and didn't like being away from my dad. I knew after being told off harshly by the girlfriend that the closed bedroom door absolutely signified 'do not disturb'.

Strangely, although I don't recall their names, or thankfully their faces, I still hear their voices in my head. Their games were not games that I was used to in any way. They involved me lying half naked under the bed wondering what this game was truly all about. I can still feel the dust and grime, see the metal mattress support on the bed and register my boredom as they half undressed me and abused me.

I don't remember feeling sadness or guilt, only confusion and a knowing that I couldn't and shouldn't tell anyone because it might make my dad cross. They were nice to me afterwards and gave me sweets and I guess at the tender age of three that must have made me quite happy.

I know that at some point my body must have reacted to the stimulation with an orgasm. This took me many years in adulthood to realise that my body was just reacting to stimuli, that I couldn't control it and that it really didn't mean that I enjoyed the abuse.

I wondered for many years why I cried and nearly had a panic attack during an orgasm as the memories of the abuse and guilt flooded my head. I don't remember when we stopped seeing the boys, but I know that I was immensely glad that we didn't go to their house anymore. We went back to spending time in our three bedroomed council, terraced home which we had shared with my mother before she had left.

Chapter 2 Child of the Seventies

I was growing up in the mid-seventies as a child living alone post-divorce with my father. He and my mother had married in 1973 and were divorced eighteen months later when she tired of his violent and controlling ways and left the family home to be with another man.

He had tried desperately to constrain and tame her wild and feisty nature, but to no avail. She did drugs, danced, partied and ran away from home before she married him and into the pregnancy and marriage this continued. There were violent assaults and sexual abuse and now, sitting here as a grown woman I can't ever blame her for leaving him. I would have done the same, however I would have taken my child with me.

Unfortunately, when my mother left the home when I was eighteen months old, I was used by my father as a pawn in a bitter divorce battle. My father allegedly denied my mother access as a punishment for her leaving him and he fought a long hard battle in court, slandering my mother's name to court workers and in divorce papers so that eventually she gave up fighting for me and agreed with him having what was known back then as custody of me. He hated my mother from the day she left him, and this dark hatred stayed with him through-out his life.

That was the start of what was to be my harrowing childhood. My early memories are traumatic and often absent, save for the ones which haunt me though to present day and which I have learned to live with and not allow to control me.

I remember sounds and smells much more than events, and I believe that quite often the brain shelters trauma in order to protect itself, and that this may be the reason that I remember so little about my childhood.

Chapter 3 The Prison

When I was around 5 my father began to date another woman. She had no children of her own and stayed at our small, grimy council house most nights. The bedroom door was locked early on and they wouldn't come out until the following day. It was lonely, and I was often hungry and sad.

I remember dragging my duvet onto the landing outside the bedroom door to sleep on many occasions just to feel that I was nearer the only human presence in the house.

Our 1970s council house was a terraced row of three-bedroom properties, and ours was sparse and bare. My father ever irresponsible with money, failed to pay the rent and despite warnings, the bailiffs came to the property twice.

They stripped the house clean of all furniture leaving only a cooker and my bed. They even took my Paddington Bear curtains and bedding. I absolutely adored Paddington and could not understand why those men came into our house to take our possessions.

I remember being interviewed by the local news agency who had been contacted to cover the story, but at four or five and not really grasping the true severity of the situation, I was bewildered by all the attention. The TV station even showed up, and while my father protested his innocence I stood and said my name when asked.

My father, who remained unable to take responsibility for his actions throughout his whole life reveled in the media furor, slating the council for instructing court action in the matter of his arrears. He could never see that he had to abide by the laws of the land, and that he was not exempt from them.

It was around this time that my fear of being left alone worsened. I remember being fast asleep in my warm bed. I woke up and instantly realised that the house felt different. I lay stock still willing my brain to work out what it was that 'felt' different. There was no noise.

That was it. My door was slightly ajar, and I could see a fraction of light spilling up through from the lounge. The TV which was normally on was off. The house was silent. With trepidation I landed both feet on the threadbare, cold carpet and pulled my pyjamas straight.

'Dad' I called quietly.

There was no response. Every hair was raised on my small skinny arms and my heart beat fast. Something was wrong.

I crept downstairs and waited at the bottom. On the wall to my side were glass fishing globes and a faux fishing net. Their presence reassured me, yet the silence petrified me.

'Dad', I tried again. Perhaps he had fallen asleep on the sofa.

I padded up the short hall and into the living room with its brown sofa and gaudy curtains. The sofa was empty, the TV off and the curtains wide open, leaving the darkness of the night there to taunt me.

I turned on my heel and moved to the front door. Despite being told not to open the front door, I gingerly tried the front door. It did not budge as I rocked on the handle. I was alone. The house was cold, silent and I was 5 and alone. Tears flowed down my freckled cheeks as I wondered what was going to happen to me.

I needed to pee but was too scared to go back upstairs to the loo. There was a downstairs loo, but that was dark and scary, and desperate I crouched down by the stairs carpet and peed where I stood. I shivered as the warm pool, quickly cooled and dried onto my little feet.

Feeling better I began to plot my escape. Venturing into the kitchen, sobbing loudly I dragged the solid wooden pitch chair over to the work top. It was hard work as I moved it level with the cupboards. I climbed nimbly up from the chair to the work top and knelt on the top, looking out into the dark night.

There was no-one around, other houses were dark, and the streetlights beckoned me onwards. I knew that I would feel safe once I was outside where other grown-ups may be, and that it was better than being afraid and alone in this scary, quiet prison.

Using two small hands I managed to free the window catch and peered out as the window opened. I was of athletic build and was often found upside down doing gymnastics, so the fear of jumping out of the window on the ground floor was not one that crossed my mind.

I swung my legs over the metal rim of the frame, brushing my legs in the process and threw myself down to the grass below the kitchen window.

It was wet under foot. As my feet got used to the feel of the cold dew on my toes, I realised that I was now stuck outside in the scary world of grown-ups, in the dark, without shoes on. It was cold, and I remember blowing dragons with my breath, watching as the air rose out of my mouth.

Praying that I would not be seen, I quietened my sobs and made my way slowly down the path. I did not have a clue where I was heading, only that being outside was preferable to the silence and fear I felt locked in the house.

I crossed the small road into our close and made my way up the main estate road. My feet hurt from the rough tarmac and I saw not a soul. I can still re-live the tight constriction of my chest as I fought the urge to scream loudly, how I jumped at every owl hooting and every bat flitting. I heard cars in the distance, but not one human came my way.

Feet raw, I covered what I now know to be around 500 metres before I saw a figure coming towards me. I was between lamp posts and the light was dimmed. I stood stock still.

Was this a stranger? A kidnapper? One of those nasty people who would take me away and hurt me? I heard a whimper and then a howl leave my lips as they approached faster now.

Suddenly I was scooped up.

'Dan, what on earth are you doing out here?' My father asked angrily.

Unable to speak through uncontrollable crying I held him tight as he carried me back to the prison and unlocked the door. I was placed back into my bed with no explanation as to his whereabouts, and do not know to this day where his late-night wanderings had taken him.

I still have terror about waking up in a house alone and fight the urge to cry if I fall asleep in bed and wake up alone when I would normally be expecting my husband to be in bed next to me. Such a short and seemingly insignificant event has imprinted itself deeply into my memory and my psyche.

Chapter 4 A New Mum

My new stepmother tried to like me, and I was desperate beyond belief to make her like me. I needed a mother figure and frankly didn't mind who it was so long as they showed me a little attention and were fairly nice. I was easily pleased and was pleased as punch when the relationship between my father and his new girlfriend intensified over time and they looked for a house together.

This resulted in us moving areas, away from the council estate and into a Victorian terraced house in a lovely area. How posh were we! Away from the grotty area and into the suburbs. The house had a cellar which had steep brick steps in, and a long back garden which I loved playing in. Out through the garage was a back alley where the kids would convene for games and fights!

There was no heating and ice froze to the inside of the windows in the winter. There was an upstairs bathroom accessed through the main bedroom and I had the bright front room. I don't remember feeling delighted that we had moved as I had to move schools to a popular primary school in an affluent area and leave my friends behind.

I was a shy yet polite kid who was desperate to work hard. I was slim in build with mousy brown scraggy hair and green almond shaped eyes with long lashes. I was immensely trusting and was desperate to make friends in my new school. I realised early on that my home life was quite different from the lives of the other privileged kids in the school and that I had little in common with them.

Ever astute, I realised that being good got me some positive attention with teachers and I settled well at school. I remember making myself look clean and tidy as I knew that I would fit in better with the other children in this middle-class primary school. Indeed, my friends at school had large houses, parents with businesses, they played instruments, danced and went on holidays. I loved going to their plush, clean houses for tea and being made a fuss of.

At home however, things were not so good. The relationship between my live-in stepmother and I was fractious, and she often resented my very being. I was told more often than not to 'shut up' and 'stop singing' and that I was too much like my own mother. I felt unloved and was often found staring at mums in the street who hugged and smiled at their children in sheer wonder. I was never jealous of them, I don't think I have the capacity even now to feel jealousy, I just wanted the same to happen to me.

My own mother had, by this time had two more children by her second husband. I loved my baby brother so, so much and used to see my mum on contact visits until she moved away to Wales when I was six or seven. I don't remember feeling part of that household, or that my mum and I had a close relationship. I don't remember missing her much initially, because I was never told that she was moving away. I know now that my father made it difficult for my mother to see much of me and thought for a long time that she'd just given up on trying. Who could blame her, I used to think!

My memories are few and far between in reality of us spending much quality time together, but I do remember that on what I think was my 6th birthday, she bought me a bright yellow Boxer bike. You know the type, with a curved saddle, high handle bars and real brakes. It was my pride and joy. I zoomed up and down the close where she lived and felt that I was important and that she must now love me as she had bought me something so wonderful.

My mother was simply stunning in my eyes. Dark curly hair (when it wasn't dyed some crazy colour), green eyes and a bubbly, effervescent personality. For as long as I could remember I knew that she was strong, brave and could stand up and fight for what she wanted. I considered her my superhero. She was a people person, and everyone loved her.

She expressed her wild and outlandish ways through her demeanor and her appearance. I remember being horrified when she dyed her hair a vibrant red and had it braided. I think even back then that I just wanted her to be like the other mums that I saw. They wore 'normal' clothes and behaved outwardly to their young charges in a loving and nurturing way.

I can only remember her collecting me from school on one occasion but remember that feeling of absolute joy when upon coming out of my reception class she was waiting by the gates. The excitement and joy as we went to the shops after school on the way to her home was intangible. Whilst I am able to recall and relive the joy felt that day, it makes me feel so sad to know that for the whole of my life at school I can only remember my mum picking me up once.

This has impacted upon my desire to drop off and collect my own children from school as I love the way that they run to me, like I have been gone from them for an eternity, rather than just one school day. I love the disheveled hair, untucked shirt and the incessant chatter that comes with the end of the school day as they recall for me their highlights. This time for me is priceless, a rite of passage synonymous with being a mother, and a time which now, I wish I could have found in my head happier memories.

At some point the contact time with my mum ceased. I can't remember a date or time, but I know it stopped. I know that I was confused, bereft and sad. I know that I cried for my mum and that it left me wanting and needing to be loved by my mother figure even more.

I was immensely lucky however to have two guardian angels in my life. I am aware that my maternal grandmother 'Nanny W' and Arty (childlike speak for aunty which stuck) my maternal aunt, were two of the most influential and loving factors in my life.

My nan was a beautiful, well-spoken and intelligent woman who loved to dance, sing and worked in a solicitors. She smoked Carlton Long cigarettes and idolised me. It's true, she absolutely doted upon me.

From the time I was five until I was eight, every weekend I would pack a small bag with my clothes and my father would drive me the short distance to my nan's home.

Her house smelled of her talcum powder and her bath was lined on the outside with aquarium effect fablon. You wouldn't believe the joy I got from sitting in her bath in her warm bathroom and playing with my plastic fish. The house was warm, with soft towels and plenty of food. The complete antithesis to my home.

Next to her twin beds were brass bear lamps, a black car ashtray and sitting menacingly in the corner of the room was Olly The Alligator, a stuffed alligator which had been taxidermy into a standing position and two creepy looking leprechauns (I still have these on my shelf of beauty and they will always have an affectionate place in my heart). My single bed was next to hers and in the winter was fitted with a cosy electric blanket. I slept soundly and deeply at her house, safe in the knowledge that I was safe, loved and cherished.

She made me cold, skinless sausages and sliced white cabbage and silver skin baby pickled onions for supper which was my favourite meal by far, and she let me paint her nails and style her hair. I was allowed on a Saturday morning to buy a packet of the fake candy sweet cigarettes and pretended to smoke them while she smoked her real ones. You might find it surprising to know that in all my life I have never even taken a drag on a real cigarette!!

We danced to rock and roll music and she taught me to jive. She absolutely loved to dance and had supposedly twisted her rib jitterbugging with an American GI soldier during the war. Her wide collection of records, many from the musicals of the 1950s and 60s were my favourite past-time and I knew every word to the songs.

Dressed up in one of her many ballroom or Latin American dancing dresses I danced and twirled, jumped and spun. With her I was encouraged to sing and dance, dress up and be a child. It was a far cry from the bleak, soulless house that I called home.

I wondered exactly why it was that I could remember so much of the time spent with my nan, and I believe that because it was such a positive experience that my memory has allowed me to remember much more of my time in her presence than the other traumas that I suffered. The human brain has an amazing capacity to block out an event and even make us forget that abuse has happened. I did not ever tell anyone at the time about my abuse, despite knowing that it was wrong, for fear that no one could actually help or that it may make my life worse.

My aunt was my mum's younger sister. They were like chalk and cheese. One blonde, one dark, one feisty, one placid, but both I considered to be my mum but for many different reasons. My aunt was a contemplative woman with a real artistic flair, a cat called Piawacket and the ability to teach me silly, nonsensical rhymes that had been passed down through generations of my family.

She would sit me on her lap on the swing in the garden and sing 'down by the river where the green grass grows, there sits Dani washing her toes, Dani, Dani won't you come to tea, come next Saturday at half past three'. I can still feel the sun on my face and the rush of air as we went higher and higher on the wooden swing. She taught me to swing on the swing on my own and encouraged creativity and expression. I loved her with all of my heart, and still do.

When my mum left my father, I spent a huge amount of time with my aunt. She was living with my nan and because of this I developed a strong bond with her.

At 18 she took me to Dawlish Warren, a popular Devon holiday resort in a caravan with her friend for a week. By all accounts I drove them both crazy asking continually where my neenee was. (My neenee was actually my dummy) My aunt spoke fondly of this holiday and I think this cemented our bonds. She became my carer, my friend, confidante and saviour.

As I got older, I was openly looking for a mother figure in any female that I met. Whether it was a teacher, neighbour, school friends mum or the lady in the corner shop. I idolised one of my best friends grandma who spoke kindly to me and told me that she would adopt me if she could. How my heart jumped for joy at the thought that I might be able to live with this kind old lady. In my head, aged around eight years old adoption was simple and I figured that she would just tell my dad that I was going to live with her!! It took a good while for me to realise that this was never going to happen.

The next best thing to a real mother was my aunt and she fitted the bill ideally. I began to think of her in a maternal way and plan ways that I may be able to live with her or my nan permanently. She was fair, honest and caring in an understated way. There was routine in her house which was a far cry from the disorder of my home. There was a beautiful blue bathroom, warm fluffy towels folded in three in the airing cupboard and central heating in every room.

Saturday morning was always wash day, and the washing machine and tumble dryer would purr away incessantly as reams of clean, soft, delightful smelling washing would emerge to find a place on the formica kitchen table. It was neatly folded into piles; my nans, my cousins, my aunts and mine. You cannot imagine how much it meant for me to have my own washing pile at her house. For me it signified having a place in the home and a feeling of belonging.

To this day I still get enormous satisfaction at tumble drying my washing and folding it into neat piles. I would have to admit to you at this point that I am horribly pedantic with towel folding and have been known to refold towels that are not folded into three with two rounded edges facing the door of my airing cupboard. I can only put this down to the feeling of calm and order that came from seeing my aunt's kitchen table and airing cupboard sporting towels folded in this manner and what it represented to me.

Saturday night entailed a bath or shower followed by a delicious tea of maybe baked mackerel, meat loaf and jacket potatoes or even fish and chips from the chip shop. These meals were eaten whist chatting and laughing with the A Team, Knight Rider or Air Wolf in the back ground. I have read that the olfactory system evokes the most memories and can absolutely relate to this judging by the happy and contented feeling that meat loaf and jacket potatoes with peas and ketchup gives me.

Chapter 5 Can't Buy Me Love

All too soon the weekend would be over, and on a Sunday afternoon I would head from the happy house back to the immensely sad and bleak one.

My stepmother would barely speak with me, save to sneer, mock or tell me off. Consequently, I spent most of time up in my room where I could shut out the hard stares, where with its half-laid carpet it was a small sanctuary. Hours were spent reading Enid Blyton and Malory Towers tales wishing desperately that I could escape to boarding school like the characters in the stories.

Their lives seemed so exciting and fun filled compared to mine that they provided me with an outlet to the misery that occurred when I went down the stairs.

It became apparent to me that if I did things for my stepmother that she was a little kinder to me. I look back upon my eight-year-old self with pity now, realising just how desperate I must have been to be loved.

I cleaned like a demon, hoovering and polishing, wiping and cleaning the kitchen floor, washing up and drying up and cleaning the bathroom. These tasks that would take me a few hours, were worth the time as they seem to get me a small reprieve for a short time. In the school holidays it was deemed that I would only be allowed out once I had completed my chores. While I listened to the laughs and shrieks of my friends, I felt like Cinderella minus the fairy godmother.

Friends were not welcome in our house and in all honesty, I was reluctant to invite them. A favourite trick of hers to ensure that they didn't want to come back ever again, was to set me a job to do whilst they were in the house. It would be washing up, hoovering or some other task that could always have waited until my friend had gone.

I realised how bored and perplexed my friends must have been by this strange behaviour, never being offered a drink or a friendly hello and can now see why I stopped inviting them into this comical world and why they never asked to come back again.

By the same vain I loved going to my friend's houses. Their parents all seemed to dote on each other and their children. There were positive affirmations and encouragement along with so much fun. Their parents would let them choose what they wanted for tea when a friend came around and never once did I see my friends have to wash up or hoover while I was there.

I was always the modicum of helpfulness when visiting in others houses, offering to wash up, clear the plates or help wherever I could, thinking all the time that they might like me more if they realised just what a helpful girl I was.

I know that I truly hoped that someone would like me enough to ask me to spend more time with them and their families, or maybe even allow me to live with them! How naïve I was.

In my desperation to be loved and approved of by my stepmother I tried to buy her love and approval. I had a large extended family who on my birthday would send me some money in a card. On my ninth birthday I was lucky enough to receive £24.

This was so much money for a little girl in the early 80's and I had planned what I might do with it. I was desperate for a number of toys that my friends all had which I really coveted. There ranged from a Cabbage Patch Kid, a My Child Doll and a Speak and Spell, an early electronic game.

On a Thursday night my dad would go out to play squash at the local sports centre. I hated being left alone with my stepmother to be picked upon or ignored but I was not allowed to go with my dad and thus became resigned to the fact that Thursday evening would become just as hideous as every other day.

That is when I came up with a cunning plan to make my stepmother respond more favourably to me. I would offer to buy her yummy sweets and snacks from the corner shop which was only nine doors from our terraced house and this would make Thursday evenings better.

And this is what I did. I asked her if she wanted anything from the shop and then went scurrying off to purchase her list of items. I would come back with a bulging sack of treats and dish them out to her and me. My plan worked and every Thursday once my dad had gone out, I would repeat the ritual of buying her love with sweets and crisps.

Within a month my precious funds were gone and I realised that I had no more bribery tools left to call upon. Unsurprisingly, without the dangling carrot of treats on hand to curb her behaviour she resumed her old revolting ways.

Chapter 6 Violence

As a small child I did not realise how warped the dynamics were between my father and stepmother. I heard him frequently speak ill about my mother, with him often telling me that she was unreliable and didn't keep her promises when it came to seeing me. He was a natural flirt with all women and seemed to consider them to be conquests, or there for him to ogle and abuse.

Throughout my younger years he had innumerable affairs which he always told me about and so an already precarious relationship became steadily worse. I wanted to gloat to my stepmother that he had taken me to someone's house and tell her that I liked her more, but I knew that he would deny it and it would be pouring oil on already troubled waters.

One Sunday evening when my sister was quite small, he had left the house to supposedly play squash. I had sat downstairs watching Falcon Crest in front of the fire which was the only heating method downstairs, while my stepmother remained upstairs. I felt so grown up turning off the TV and putting myself to bed somewhere after 10pm.

I awoke to the most terrified, blood curdling screams coming from downstairs. I could hear my father swearing and screaming at my stepmother and her in response crying and asking him to stop whatever it was he was doing to her. I lay so still, unable to move a muscle. My heart beat ferociously in my chest and I cried silent tears down my face onto my pillow. My hands shook, and I sweated. I desperately wanted to be brave enough to go downstairs to use the phone to call someone to come and make the screaming stop, but terror incapacitated me totally.

I heard my stepmother break free from my father's clutches and make for the stairs. Her frantic steps on the steep wooden staircase were stopped as he grabbed her by the hair and pulled her back down. I heard her thud as she hit the wall at the bottom of the stairs and the screaming began again in earnest as he began to drag her around the red tiled floor of the tiny kitchen. She cried and screamed as he beat her, and I heard her sobbing as her ankle was cut open.

To this day I am petrified of loud screaming and shouting. My hackles rise in terror and take me back to that evening when I was forced to pee in the corner of my room in terror rather than risk going downstairs to the bathroom and witnessing first-hand the carnage that had ensued.

How on earth the neighbours didn't call the police I will never know. I guess the mentality in the early 80's was not to interfere in your neighbours business knowing that the probable response from the police would have been to label the abuse as a domestic and side with the perpetrator.

The following morning my stepmother showed me her bruises, hair loss and lacerated ankle. She told me that she had pretended to have left the house and had been hiding in the cellar when my father returned from squash having had a few bevvies in the bar. She wanted I guess to make him think that she had left alone a new baby and me, who was around nine years of age. I was thoroughly traumatised and confused by the violence and didn't get at all the seriousness of the attack.

I witnessed my father's manipulation first hand when he appeared with a shoddy bunch of guilt laden flowers hoping for forgiveness for his violence. The apology meant nothing as he blamed her for making him angry in the first place, rather than taking responsibility for his own behaviour. This misogynistic behaviour continued day in, day out within the home, and the violence that I heard that night still turns my blood cold when I recall the sounds of distress and pain.

The house was fraught with arguments and back stabbing between the two adults. There was little love and affection shown to anyone bar my sister from my stepmother. It was as if the moment my sister arrived into this world that I became a non-entity in the home.

Chapter 7 A Cry for Help

The daily ritual of getting me to school was traumatic and I was almost always late. I would get myself up and ready, have breakfast and do my teeth and beg my stepmother to get up to take me to school. To walk it was around a mile in distance, but I was not allowed to walk alone. Instead I was forced to watch the time tick by as I willed my stepmother to get up out of bed and either walk me to school or drive.

More often than not she would eventually get up at 08.45, mosey around getting ready and we would set off for school around 09.00. I hated being late into class as it bought unwanted attention to me as I had to make up an excuse as to why for the third time that week I was late again.

I cried quite often on the way to school and sometimes lingered in the cloak room a while as I dried my tears and asked God for a parent to treat me like the other children in my class. How I envied those lucky children whose parents held their hand on the way to school, kissed them and hugged them as they bid them farewell for the day, made them school lunches with hand chosen items that they knew their children would love and collected them with a cheery smile at the end of the day.

Sadly, none of this came to pass and in fact my life was to get a whole lot worse.

I heard from my mother infrequently after she moved to South Wales to begin a new relationship, and I was desperate for any sort of contact with her. The calls and the letters that she promised when she saw me never materialised.

The Monday night phone calls that she had promised came for two weeks and then gradually faded away. I would wait by the phone at the given time willing it to ring. No amount of will made it ring and I would retreat to my bedroom to sob. I would sit on my bed or the floor and wonder just what it was about me that had made my mum move so far away and my stepmother to clearly hate me.

The loneliness that I felt even aged nine was all encompassing. It was made worse by the continued emotional abuse perpetrated by my stepmother as she sought to torment me and put me down. She especially enjoyed taunting me about my mother's inability to keep her promises, 'Your mum doesn't care about you' she would say as I waited patiently for the phone to ring. When I conceded that the phone was not going to ring she would continue her vile tirade, 'I told you she never phones, she's forgotten about you' she spat.

I look back now and conclude that I was quite depressed. I cried every day at school but had no one to seek help from. I tried to be happy and bubbly like my friends but found myself bursting into tears frequently and confiding in my friends just how horrible my life at home was. My friends felt sorry for me, I know that much, and a few told their parents. Back in the 80's few people got involved with other people's business and safe guarding amongst the general public was not heard of nor encouraged.

With no other route out, I began to think about killing myself as I deduced that things would never get better and that most people didn't care if I was alive or dead. It was with this thought in my mind that I plotted just how I would commit suicide. I don't think I wanted to actually die, as in end my life, but would have settled for someone to rescue me. I guess it was a cry for help.

I had been given a sturdy black leather purse come bag by my nan and it had a thick strap attached. It wasn't a very attractive thing, purely functional.

I planned that I could hang the purse around my neck with the strap twisted and then suspend it from the coat pegs in the cloak room, effectively strangling myself.

On yet another miserable morning, after a torrent of abuse and being late yet again I could take no more. The cloak room was empty, it was 09.15 on the clock and my class must have filed into the main hall to assembly. My classroom was next door to the cloak room and the silence was strangely comforting.

With tears streaming once again down my freckled cheeks I wound the leather strap of my purse come bag over the coat peg. Next, I slipped my head through the loop and lifted my feet from the floor. A brief feeling of pressure encased my neck and I willed the end to come swiftly.

Without warning the leather strap broke away from the purse and sent me reeling forward onto my knees on the floor of the tiled cloak room. The coat peg was nearly out of the wooden housing and I was left in a snotty heap on the floor. I sat and cried in sheer frustration. I didn't know who to turn to or what to do to make my situation better, but I knew at that moment that I had reached my first turning point. I couldn't change my home situation at all at the tender age of nine, but I would begin to fight back in my own way.

I realised that I wouldn't be young forever and that even at that young age, I was aware that I could in years to come have more control over my future. This is where my resourcefulness and resilience truly began.

Chapter 8 The Carpet

My father was one of those men who would start a job and never finish it. This was never truer than when he laid a carpet in my bedroom. The beige carpet was half laid with the rest of the roll still present in my room over 1 year later. My room was quite small but immaculately kept. I loved order in my chaotic life. I think it helped to frame who I am today.

Fastidious in my tidiness the carpet however annoyed the life out of me. The roll was cumbersome in its size and took up vital space. So, during an uneventful and boring school holiday I decided that I would lay the carpet myself. I had watched closely as my father made his first attempt at laying the carpet and I knew the tools that I would need!

A trip down to the untidy shed to find some tacks was successful. The super sharp and slightly scary Stanley knife and hammer proved to be more evasive. A good deal of searching located the Stanley knife, yet the hammer, vital to my task remained elusive! I slipped a butter knife in my pocket as I felt it might be useful to tuck the carpet under the skirting board.

Undeterred I improvised with a saucepan in place of a hammer and set off back upstairs, excited to be changing my room for the better.

I believe that this was the start of my 'can-do' attitude and my awareness that I could be more in control of my world. To this day I am happy to always have a go and learn as I go along, whether that's a practical job or new skill.

So, picture this; my skinny nine-year-old self began to move the furniture. I was trying to be quiet as I moved the bed as I knew that I shouldn't be doing this at all. Thankfully my room was small, and my pieces of furniture were scanty, and possessions were even scarcer.

Bed and chest of drawers moved, I began to push the carpet towards the wall as tight as I could get it. I had watched my father do exactly the same thing when he laid the carpet around the other 3 walls thus felt quite confident that I knew what to do!!

Once it was as tight as I could get it (not tight at all, given that I was around 4 stones) I gingerly slid out the blade of the knife. Have you ever been tempted to touch a knife to see how sharp it is? I was magnetically drawn to the pointed tip of the blade as I plucked up the courage to start to cut.

Starting in the middle of the wall I slid the knife into the foam backed carpet. The knife glanced through it like it was butter. Taking care to keep my fingers out of the way I pushed the edge firmly into the skirting and continued with my cutting.

It was not long until I had worked my way from one side of the room to the other. Overjoyed I sat, exhilarated and confident that I could now complete the task in hand. Taking the sharp tacks from my pocket I made sure the edge of the carpet (a little wonky in places) butted up to the skirting board. Then, taking a tack I pressed it into the carpet and gave it an almighty smack with my stolen saucepan. The sound echoed loudly around the room but thankfully the bottom of the saucepan showed no signs of its toil. Spacing my tacks out evenly I continued my work until each tack was embedded in the soft floor boards.

One final task lay in trying to push the carpet under the skirting board to make the edges match those on the other three sides of the room. This I accomplished by using the butter knife to poke the edge under the small gap between the skirting. Painstakingly I lay on my belly, meticulously neatening my carpet. Once finished I sat awestruck at what I had accomplished. I moved the remnant role up onto my bed and studied the overall effect that this seemingly insignificant task had made upon my little room.

My room looked larger and tidier, however the largest overall effect was not what was physically noticeable in the room, but what changed that day within me.

For the first time I felt powerful and in control for a short space of time. My confidence was sky rocked and I longed for the next challenge. My attitude to obstacles and challenges was such that nothing, not even the later hardships which were to occur later in my childhood, could dampen my will to be in control of my life and overcome whatever hurdles were sent my way.

As you will see, there have been many, many circumstances which were ugly, harrowing and traumatic. Please, believe me when I say that I would not change a minute of my life thus far as I believe that it has made me into the resilient, strong and focused woman that I am today.

If you are facing obstacles and challenges in your life, no matter how small, I want you to know that you can change things and endure more than you thought possible. You are stronger than you think.

Chapter 9 Let's Play Tickle

My joy in my accomplishments was short lived however and the negative and unhappy situation continued with its challenges.

My stepmother had parents who lived a short drive from our home. They had never really warmed to me, and my stepmother told me they hated my father, believing that he was not the best choice in a breeding partner for their daughter. As a mother myself I was most inclined to agree! What parent wants their child to be in a relationship with a controlling and abusive person?

They had a yappy poodle who barked and growled at me and made me feel even more ill at ease and clearly felt the same as the step-grandparents. From the moment I entered the house I felt sick. My hands would shake, and my stomach would churn with butterflies. The hairs on my arms stood up and I became hyper-vigilant.

Back then I could never understand just why those feelings emerged, but after the events that occurred one day when I was sent to stay there, I realise that my intuition was in tune with my environment and was working overtime to warn me.

I have learnt huge amounts about intuition and self-preservation in my adult years, but I absolutely cannot recall when I consciously began to trust that voice inside me which told me that a situation, person or place was unsafe, hostile or dangerous. Sadly, the younger me had no way of extracting myself from the situation that arose that one day, despite my little voice screaming loudly that things were very wrong indeed.

It was the summer holidays and I had been sent to my step-grandparents for the day whilst the adults worked. It was a typical summers day, with balmy blue skies and the sun shining down. I loved to stay outside and play in the garden, but the step-grandfather was overtly precious about his garden and hated me running around, thus in order to keep the peace I was confined indoors.

I had taken things to do but had exhausted them and had taken to doing handstands in the living room. The room was empty and plenty large enough for me to practice my skills. I was a budding gymnast and spent more time upside down that I did on two feet. The living room was dark and musty, because the curtains were often half shut and smelt of musty dog. I hated that room with a vengeance.

I know that I was wearing a skirt and can see the room clearly in my head. At the top end of the room was a high-backed chair where the step-grandfather sat. It was his chair and his chair only. There was a sofa to the side of this and the TV was in the corner of the room. I recall it was quite dark in the room and the curtains were drawn slightly despite the sun outside.

So, there I was, Nadia Comaneci in the making, upside down, skirt tucked into my knickers when in walked the step-grandfather. He closed the white door shut tight and walked over to his chair. 'Carry on doing your handstands, it's ok, I'll watch you' he said.

As an adult, I look back on those few minutes and wonder why I didn't trust my instinct and leave the room. Was I expecting this to happen after my earlier experiences of abuse? Did I believe that I was deserving of this kind of attention?? I can't honestly say.

When he was done watching my handstands he spoke again, 'let's play a game' he said 'it's called tickle.'

I immediately felt uncomfortable but was reluctant to be labelled as more difficult and challenging than my stepmother had already told them I was. So, the good girl in me, anxious to please agreed to this strange game.

'You need to sit on my knee' he coaxed part lifting me onto his lap.

And so, the game commenced. It involved him tickling me around my middle and over my un-developed chest. It felt alien to be so close to someone who had barely paid me any attention previously and now wanted to be my new best friend.

As I struggled against his relentless tickles, he began to tickle my legs, my knees and my stomach. My short skirt was no barrier to his wandering hands as they began to brazenly tickle the tops of my legs under my skirt. I knew that this was not a game that I should be playing but felt powerless to ask him to stop and did not know how to deal with his behaviour.

Eventually both hands were around the top of my thighs near to my knickers. I froze. My legs were stuck apart either side of his, with his hands burrowing now into my knickers towards my private, not so private parts.

Those seconds seemed like hours as I was rigid with fear as he tickled my vagina. I did not move a muscle. I cannot remember thinking anything. I was mute and virtually catatonic. Sudden footsteps in the hall brought me back to the present and startled him enough that he swiftly moved his hands from under my skirt to round my middle as the door handle moved.

In walked his wife, the step-grandmother. The tickling continued for show for a few moments before I wriggled free and bolted for the door. I was unable to comprehend exactly what had really happened moments before, I scuttled out through the kitchen to the relative safety of the garden.

In the days and hours that passed, I mused as to why that horrible thing had happened. I concluded that I must have made the grandfather and the older boys believe that I wanted it to happen and that they knew that I was bad and dirty.

If only I could tell my younger self that it was not my fault and that I didn't give off 'abuse me' signals. These people clearly saw a vulnerable, lonely little girl and knew that she would have trouble finding someone to protect her.

From that day onwards, I never went into the deeper recesses of the house, staying politely in the kitchen or in the off-limits garden. My instinct was developed enough to know that I would be in heaps of trouble if I was to be left alone in his company again.

Chapter 10 Birthdays

My 4th birthday was one of the most memorable days of my life. A party was held at my nanny's and a few little friends came along. I don't remember my mum or dad being there, but my aunt and nan hosted. The party was held in my nan's dining room around her huge, wooden table which looked the size of a ship to a small child.

The table was laden with cheese and pineapple stuck into half an orange, sausages on sticks, jam sandwiches and fairy cakes. Even to this day I love a good party tea with all the 70's trimmings.

This was the first birthday that I remember, and I recall much laughter and fun. The highlight however, was the cake, it was a bunny sleeping in a bed and was intricate in its making. I have no idea who conceived the idea of two cute bunnies laid in a bed, with a blanket, pillow and teddy, but it was super cute. It was the most beautiful thing that I had ever seen, and I couldn't believe that it was mine.

My aunt, ever the tease, brought the cake to the table with four blazing candles. Happy birthday was sung, and the cake was taken away to be cut, ready to be consumed by the hungry hordes.

My aunt left the room carrying my beautiful cake, then doubled back. I saw at the last minute the sharp knife that she carried in her hand and assumed that it was to cut generous slices of cake for us to eat. I couldn't have been more wrong, as with a wicked glint in her eye she pretended to saw off the sugar icing bunny heads. Well, my inner demon was absolutely unleashed, and I began to scream and stamp.

Crying hysterically, I ran up to her and kicked her hard in the shin, anything to stop her from decapitating my bunnies. At that my aunt relinquished the knife, thudded the cake down on the table and removed my screeching form from the dining room, much to the amusement of my neighbours and friends. I was suitably chastised and in a poignant photo from that afternoon I look quite forlorn.

Birthdays as I got older were not however full of fun and laughter. With little contact from my mum, bar occasionally a week in the summer holidays, I grew to accept that I couldn't spend my actual birthday with her but was stuck in the morose environment to which I had become accustomed. On my birthday morning, I would rush downstairs hoping that my day would be filled with love, hugs and presents.

Sadly, this was not the case. Invariably my stepmother would not acknowledge that it was my birthday and my father would completely forget. I remember him disappearing up to the corner shop to buy a card, writing it hurriedly in the kitchen afterwards and popping a £5 note inside. As I watched him write the card and pop the money inside, I wanted ungratefully to tell him to not bother, that I knew what was inside the card thus the surprise was over.

Back then I loved surprises and still will hold out with presents and plans to give my kids well thought out surprises and gifts.

My friends had such pomp and circumstance on their birthdays, with sleep overs, party tea, balloons and streamers and a hoard of presents. I dreamed every year of this being how my birthday panned out, yet the dream seldom came.

On yet another birthday my father appeared with my present which had been bought at around 10am on my birthday from the newsagents up the road. It was wrapped in a paper bag and was a cheap, plastic dolls head with a tiny comb and some rollers. I remember feeling heartbroken that he had forgotten once again, and that on what was meant to be my special day, it passed without so much as a balloon, cake or kind wish.

On my 12th birthday the local shop provided him with a bright yellow umbrella which he gave me as I left for school. It was hideous and still had the label on it from Johnson's Newsagents. Why my stepmother couldn't have reminded him that my birthday was coming up I will never, ever know. It was just another way of showing me that I was hated and a lesser person than the other two children in the household.

Back in those days the post arrived early, and with great gusto I would rush down the steep Victorian staircase as soon as I heard the rattle of the post-box. Invariably there would be cards from my great aunt, my godmother, my great gran, my maternal and paternal grandparents, but more often than not, missing from in amongst that pile of cards was a card from my mum and siblings in Wales.

I would go off to school heartbroken. The feelings of shear isolation and desertion weighed me down. I would often spend the day in tears, feeling embarrassed that yet again my birthday had no special meaning. All that I wanted in the world was a card or phone call from my mum and my dad. I knew that my younger sister's birthday was the day before mine and that my mother couldn't realistically forget mine.

When I was around nine the card from my mum arrived a good number of days late. I recall that she believed that it had got delayed in the post. Eventually, the card arrived, carrying far less impact after the birthday. Inside the card was a five-pound note, with an effusive message about how much I was missed and that my mum would call or see me soon. I didn't hold on to those promises as they had a habit of being broken fairly soon after they were made.

I know now that my father was hugely obstructive with contact, yet as a child I was unable to see the wrangling which went on behind the scenes. I was however grateful for the money. I don't mean that in a mercenary way, but as a child who didn't have a lot, to receive some money for my birthday which I could spend was so special.

In deciding how to spend my five-pound birthday money I set out to find something that would remind me of my mum. Being an avid book reader, it was the obvious choice for a gift. I loved the escapism in the character's lives. How I longed to attend Malory Towers school or St Clare's, with their fun filled days and warm families.

So, a few weeks later, on a shopping trip in to our local city I happened into the Marks & Spencers store. There, enticing me, was a hard backed, scary, black, story book. It was entitled, 101 Ghost Stories. It was heavy and felt good in my hands. It was the kind of gift that I wished my mum had taken the time to choose for me.

I loved it and couldn't wait to get home to begin to read it. I wanted to acknowledge to myself that the gift was from my mum and couldn't think of a better way to do this than writing a message in the front to myself. It read 'To Dani, have a very happy birthday, with all of my love from mum.'

It was written in my neat, measured script and was littered with kisses and hearts. I absolutely wanted my mum to have chosen a book which she might have known that I would have loved, but I know now that she had no idea what books I read and how voracious my appetite was for the written word. Recalling that childish inscription today makes me feel so sad for my younger self. Desperate to be loved and acknowledged, however left feeling second best to siblings and forgotten and unloved by parents.

I grew to loathe birthday's every year, always waiting for the moment that the card or present from my mum or dad failed to arrive and always knowing that I would end up crying. I saw how other families reacted to birthday's, with special tea parties with balloons and cake, singing and presents and was desperate for a little slice of that too. I had been told how my siblings' birthdays were celebrated, with parties, home-made cake, chosen treats, well thought out presents and happiness.

Once I became a mum myself, I recreated those birthdays for my children that I'd wanted so badly as a child. Banners, huge helium balloons, singing, presents over breakfast, hugs and their choice of chosen meal for tea. I wanted them to always know that their birthday was special to us all.

My revelations into the deeper relationship between my mum and I as I approached my forties would reveal that in truth, she often forgot about me. Out of sight did in fact mean for her, out of mind. I don't blame her for it and know that we had no bonds due to circumstance, but as a child, on special occasions it was a bitter pill to swallow. As a child I was so desperate for the person who I adored and sat on a pedestal to act in a way commensurate with other mums that I refused to acknowledge the truth.

I am grateful to my aunt and nan for arranging the birthday parties that I did have. I recall being delighted with a teddy bear cake smothered in rich chocolate, lovingly made by my aunt. For my 11th birthday I was allowed to utilise the 'play room', which was the large room at the back of the house for my party. I invited many members of my class and we danced and sang until our heads hurt from the noise. I remember loving my grey circular skirt, which I wore with knee length white socks! Having the attention from my aunt and nan on these birthdays made them doubly special.

Chapter 11 Out of Sight

My mum moved to Wales when I was around seven years old. She chose to live in a beautiful, ex hippy commune near the sea, with no street lights, a bumpy track for a road in amongst some very eccentric and laid-back folks. On my first visit I was horrified. It was the complete anthesis to my world back home.

Her home was a one-story chalet with a tin roof. The back door was a stable type and looked out onto a steep, wilderness of a garden. The inside was open plan and the only internal door was a sliding one on the bathroom. The lounge had floor cushions and my three siblings shared one bedroom. Curtains portioned the bedrooms off, people wandered in and out at all hours and the open house policy continued right into the night. It was a strange, new world for me.

My life in the little Victorian house whilst unpleasant had order and structure. There was a routine and I could shut the door on the world in my bedroom. I was like a fish out of water in this world and the differences were gargantuan. I found this laissez-faire kind of existence as uncomfortable as the constriction at my home.

I was shy and found mixing with strangers difficult. The constant visitors into the house made me feel awkward and ill at ease. I did not know who to trust and who to find as a friend. Those weeks spent in the house have some happy memories yet are inflected with sadness when I recall just wanting some peace and quiet so that I could spend some time with just my mum.

I was desperate for any kind of attention from her, just for a few moments, but she was either busy looking after my three younger siblings or entertaining the many and varied folks who dropped in for tea, supper or a bed for the night.

As a child who got through the day with order and routine the lack of it was just as scary. As I slept on my bed on the floor, listening to loud music banging late into the night I felt like a complete outsider. Frightened and feeling ill at ease I longed for the normality of my friend's families, with their homely mums, tidy houses and affectionate parents.

My mother's house was no show home and had a lived-in feel. The chalet was a pre-war home, designed to get people out of the city, during the bombing that took place in WW2 and the lounge floor was adorned with large floor cushions. Meal times were a whole new entity, with lentils and TVP (Textured Vegetable Protein) on the menu. In my dad's house, we ate traditional meat and two veg kind of meals, as he refused to eat any of that 'foreign shit' as he called it, referring to pizza and lasagne!!

So, it was no surprise that I drew attention to myself as I pushed the dahl or nut roast around my plate. I was mocked for being fussy and difficult with food, and from this moment tried to demolish everything that was put before me to avoid standing out from the rest of my family. To try and fit in and gain attention, I took to doing what I did best at home during the holidays; cleaning. To show my mum what a good girl I was and how useful I could be I began a routine of hoovering, polishing, tidying up and cleaning the kitchen. It took me hours and rather than getting the response I desired, my mother looked at me like I was bonkers.

I think it drove her slightly mad that I didn't know how to be a child in this environment, that I was so used to staying safe and watching who might try and hurt me that I couldn't let my guard down. My state of vigilance and need to please continued for many years after when I was at the house. Desperate to feel part of the group, desperate to be invited to live with them, in their happy house, but knowing deep down that I didn't belong in that world.

My siblings were so at home in their house. Safe, lavished with love and attention, praised for their achievements and spoilt rotten at birthdays and Christmases. Because I only saw them once or twice a year, our relationship was strange. They knew that I was their sister, but that I didn't belong. I was staying in their rooms with my bag and they knew that I would be leaving soon. There were no photos of me on the wooden partition wall and whilst I didn't ever query that when I was a child, it became like a thorn in my side as I struggled to contemplate that I missed my mum so much more than she actually missed me.

My mother was the sort of mum that my friends idolised. Attractive, confident and very good fun. She was the instigator of mischief and tom foolery and was the one often found starting the lentil fight or leading the charge with potato guns drawn for battle. She was five feet two of lioness and loved to be the sorter out-ter of problems and flex her muscles to protect her young whenever needed.

My friends left meeting my mum, wishing that she was theirs too. I was proud to call her my mum and sat her on a pedestal so high that she became like an idol to me.

This experience of my other world gave me strength though. It allowed me to see that you didn't have to conform to the way that others wanted you to live and that with love and family around you, you could feel safe and nurtured. I looked at my siblings, their confident demeanour, feeling that they could conquer the world and that my mother would back them in their fight and desperately wanted to feel that too.

Chapter 12 Different

As a child I knew that my mother was virtually shunned by her family for her existence in the non-conformist world that she lived in. My grandmother hated her flightiness and her drive to live as she thought fit. This created a huge divide between them and made their relationship even more fractious that it had been when my mum left me with my dad. My aunt, the younger of the two sisters, who I fondly named 'Arty' was my pseudo mum. She and my mum were the complete antithesis of each other and for me she was present in my life with a regularity that my mother was not.

My aunt and mother, at that point did not see eye to eye and tolerated each other's presence for many years. My mum's way of life confused my aunt, and my mum struggled to see the appeal of a life with a 9-5 job, tidy, decorated rooms and a conventional house. The more time I spent with my aunt the more I hung onto her to fill the gaps left by my absent mother and abysmal home life.

The routine, clean bath towels, warm hugs and attention was all that I needed to make me feel less alone and scared.

The fact that my nan and aunt struggled to get on with my mum, was a source of angst for me. I really couldn't see why they had to row and hated it when my mum slated my nan. I loved my nanny with all of my being and felt torn between the two of them. My mum struggled to see just how important my nan was to me, that she was my weekend solace and I felt loved, safe and wanted when I was with her. I didn't understand until years later just why my mum resented my grandmother so much.

What I would realise was that nan absolutely favoured her younger, more conformist daughter and her family, although I believe that years later she tried to make it up to my mother. It was too little, too late. My mother stood back on the side lines and watched as my nan lavished her attention and money on me and my cousin, and virtually denied the existence of my mum and her three children. The more my nan frowned upon my mum's lifestyle choices the more exuberant she became. It was almost as if she had decided to test my nan to see just how much she could shock her and push her away completely.

As an adult I have become able to see how alike my relationship with my mum mimicked that of her and my nan. How it was ok to her to treat one of her children so differently, albeit, unintentionally and how easy it was for her to ignore me as my nan had ignored my mum. The sins of the fathers and all that jazz…..

As a mother I have always sought to maintain a bond with my children and love them with all my heart. I cannot ever imagine being in the situation whereby you leave your child and have little contact, yet don't judge those who do, for whatever reason.

Chapter 13 Uncertainty

As an adult, I have always found uncertainty stressful. I still get physical symptoms which manifest in not just butterflies in my stomach but massive pterodactyls circling in my solar plexus. I feel wobbly. Not knowing for me, or not controlling my surroundings brings on rushes of questions..... *what if? how? When? why?*.....These, along with my churning stomach, multiple trips to the loo and the crazy questions heighten my stress. As the stress worsens the birds get bigger, the churning gets worse and so the cycle grows.

As a child, my world was full of uncertainty. This is why I craved routine and hated the '*comme ci, comme ca*' world at my mother's house. At my dad's home, there was the question about how much I may be told off, how many times I would be told to 'shut up', whether I would be asked to get off the sofa because I didn't buy it, whether I would be made packed lunches for school, or had to go hungry or whether another adult was going to try and push their hands in my pants. These were my daily uncertainties and I found the never knowing 'what if' drove me bonkers.

I know with my own children, how important boundaries and routine are, and how much security it gives them when life is predictable. My hyper vigilance for arguments, screaming, changed tones and change of body language resulted in me not wanting to let go and do kid stuff.

My time was better spent watching and waiting for what may occur. I know my behaviour and inability to relax and chill drove my mum mad. Maybe if she had known my situation better then she may have understood why I was like I was and just what was going on.

As an adult, I have had to learn coping strategies to get me through situations which I just cannot control. And, trust me, I have realised that there is so much about life that you cannot control. Other people, the weather, animals, children, procedures and oh so much more.

The list is endless. In all of this I have learned that acceptance and going with the flow can make situations much less stressful. The birds still circle, but they are sparrow size nowadays. They don't dominate my being and control my thoughts.

I ask myself, 'does this matter?' and try to break down why it might not matter to me that I control the events surrounding me. In using a degree of rational thought and reasoning I can begin to challenge my outlandish thoughts and put them into perspective.

As a child I did not have the requisite skills to enable me to challenge the thoughts and capture the birds, because my world was filled with unpredictability. I realise now that we only know what we know and can only grow if we teach ourselves or are taught skills and knowledge.

Today, I enjoy using meditative breathing and focusing upon all the good things in my life to help to relax and focus my thoughts in an uncertain situation. I find that 'box breathing' or Four-square breathing helps to calm and de-stress me.

There are many different types of meditative and controlled breathing techniques. You just have to find one that works for you. In Four-square breathing you focus on counting slowly to four whilst breathing in slowly. You then hold that breath for four, before breathing out slowly for four, then holding again for four. Try and do this for a few minutes to regulate the breathing and reduce stress and anxiety.

Like all things, it takes practice and effort to make this work, but by virtue of the mechanism of breathing and slowing down your breathing rate, it will have a positive effect on the autonomic nervous system.

Sadly, as a child, in school we were not taught stress relief or any form of meditation. How valuable would that be today in our highly stressed out world?

I love the meditation and mindfulness apps that are so easily obtainable now. I find starting something new quite hard to fit in but love the ability to just sit quietly for five minutes or longer and feel the business of the brain, thoughts and questions quieten for just a moment.

Chapter 14 Blurred Lines

My father like to keep me looking young. I was encouraged to act as a little girl even as I grew up. He was not a loving, tactile father and would seek to put people down in an unkind way. There was no room for opinion in our house, unless it was that held by him, and at the meal table it was a time for eating and certainly not chatting.

I was abused by my father for many years. Thankfully, my memories, all but one bright technicolor video have faded and buried themselves so deep that I am unable to access them.

I know that I was around seven or eight when the event I strongly recall occurred. My stepmother went to work in the evening, leaving me with my father and baby sister. He would be working in the garage at the end of the garden and I would be left to put her to bed. She would cry and scream if placed into her cot and so the only way to get her to sleep would be to rock her in your arms for what seemed like an eternity.

Place her back in the cot once her eyes had closed and she would immediately sense that she had been put down and placed in the prison like bed and the whole blessed routine would start again.

I walked round and round the tiny bedroom with her in my arms, willing her to sleep, so that I could go downstairs, or back to my room.

One evening when I was in bed and my father was downstairs I heard him come up the stairs. There was a chink of light through my door from the tiny landing which cast shadows in my room, making it seem more cosy and friendly than it felt. The stairs were creaky and narrow, in typical Victorian fashion, with a tiny landing at the top of them. To the left led to the main bedroom and through bathroom, to the right was my bedroom.

My bed was placed against my mural-led wall and I heard him enter the room. I felt myself freeze, pinned to the bed, scared, but unsure why. The only light was that from the dim bulb on the landing. I am to this day unsure of how I was taken or lifted out of bed, but found myself face down on the bed with my nightdress around my waist.

I felt a hand on my back and a hand opening my legs. I played dead. I remember I didn't shout out, didn't cry, didn't move as the hands began to work up the back of my legs. I remember confusion, and resignation. This was the third person to want to touch my private parts and I didn't know how to say no, how to make it stop or even who might make it stop.

The hands, rough and probing began to touch my vagina and bottom. Murmuring as he touched and hurt me. 'Nearly there' he said. That phrase is ingrained in my memory. I remember he moved behind me, but I dared not say a word. I had no comprehension of what was nearly there or of what he was doing as he spread my bottom cheeks and touched my anus.

I have no concept of time or how the assault stopped, but I have a horrible sense that I had an orgasm. How a seven-year-old child can respond to such depraved behaviour, I really struggled with for such a long time. Guilt at how my tiny body responded and why mother nature would be so cruel evaded me for many fucked up years. The power that the orgasm, conceived out of such evil beginnings, minus love and consent has played havoc with my relationships for all of my life.

My orgasms were power enough to evoke the feelings of guilt, terror and repulsion every time. I would be transported back to that moment in time where I lay on my front powerless to stop anything. My orgasms, once consensually sexually active left me shell shocked, in a total state of panic, unable to breathe and grasping for anything in the room to grab hold of in order to ground me back to what should have been a wonderful release.

I realise now that children's bodies are no different to adults. If stimulated they may respond, as programmed to do. My later therapy gave food for thought that I had probably been sexually abused by my father many times, but thankfully there is much that I cannot, or will not remember. There is so much that I know that I have blocked out of my mind, which I feel is a blessing and which I do not need to remember in order to heal.

I knew for so many years that the relationship with my father was wrong, but as I grew older, having locked away so much I could never put my finger on just what was askew. He tried to keep control of me, banning make up and boyfriends and was always touching me, yet still I did not remember any details. I wonder if my brain did me a huge favour in my teenage years, suppressing such terrors so as to keep me on a much more even keel than had I had recollections of the abuse. I remember reading an article on survivors of sexual abuse and the rate of mental health issues and addictions.

I consider myself immensely lucky that I came through the abuse remarkably unscathed, at least on the outside. Whatever conclusions that can be drawn from abuse of children, it is that it is never, ever the child's fault. As a child I thought that I was dirty, bad and deserved the unwanted attention from men. After many years of healing and through working through what happened to me, I know now that I was never to blame for my father's perversions and choices.

Life from the age of eight is not something that I remember clearly. I remember being unhappy and wanting life to change, actual events are few and far between. I have researched why massive gaps may be present in my memories and more often than not it points to trauma and the brains protective mechanisms kicking in.

I know that I was often labelled sly and difficult and recall my stepmother telling perfect strangers that I was a bad child. I remember being massively jealous of my sister given that she received so much love, attention and care from my stepmother. I just wanted her to go away and never come back, given that I was most certainly the second best child in the house.

The constant criticism, ridicule and mental abuse played havoc with my confidence. I was desperate to be accepted, liked, and tried hard to be good at school or round at friend's houses so that their parents would like me and ask me back.

As an adult I despise unfairness and bullying, linking them back to my treatment as a child. I am often the first to step in and help the underdog and will put myself on the line in order to defend someone who is dear to me. I can feel my hackles rise up and my heart begin to rage as they did when I was the one at the receiving end of the bullying.

I often wonder why no-one ever seemed to notice that I was so unhappy at school, but I guess, that child protection back in those days was not what it is today. I was a good chameleon, I hid the abuse well. I was clean and tidy, performed well at school and was sociable, if not a little precocious.

No teacher ever noticed me asking for food from my friends! Them with their glorious lunch boxes filled with delights, when I had the same sandwich three days running because I hated what was in it and was too stupid or too honest to bin it and tell my stepmother that I had actually eaten it!

To this day I cannot abide the smell of liver pate, as it was the one and only thing that was put in my sandwiches daily, despite me hating it. I dreamt of ham and salad, chocolate spread or jam, along with a piece of fruit and a chocolate biscuit, or heaven forbid, a pot of raisins and a piece of cake!

I make such an effort with lunch boxes for my children. Tiny as it may seem I urge parental care and attention by lunch boxes! Even when I used to make six lunch boxes every night for my hoard's I would pay close attention to what I put in them. Carefully wrapping small parcels of raisins, making little plastic boxes of crudités and carefully made sandwiches, with fillings that I knew that the children would like.

I now know that I show love by doing things for those who I love. These small, seemingly insignificant actions are what I so desperately wanted as a child, and this is how I have come to judge showing someone that you love them, along with the conventional hugs and kind words. How strange is it that in a world with so many things wrong I was so hung up on lunch boxes!! In the grand scheme of things, it was the least of my worries!

Through reading and self-exploration, I know that it is OK for a loved one or partner to not show love in the same way as me. I am uber demonstrative and tactile, probably to the point of being annoying. Thankfully my husband doesn't find it so.

For many years I felt unloved by him because he didn't show affection as openly as I did. What I realise now is that he shows his love by providing for me and his family. He is a constant planner and a thinker. We are just different, and here after years of thinking, mulling over and enlightenment I am at peace with our differences.

Chapter 15 No Lock

Our tiny, bathroom was on the ground floor, just by the dark kitchen. It was freezing in the winter and it was a room that I hated for more than just one reason. I began wearing a bra when I was around eleven, and although I was completely flat chested my father loved coming into the bathroom when I was in there.

He found reason to need the loo, to wash his hands or find something in the cupboard when I was showering or washing. He would never knock, just barge in with no apology or spoken word.

It felt like he was marking his territory in more than just the physical sense of owning the room. Often if I was washing at the sink he would come in and rub my back or massage my shoulders in a way which made me so uncomfortable, yet, I stayed silent, not recalling the earlier abuse at his hands but knowing that something was desperately wrong with his actions, but not knowing how I could ask him to leave.

He refused to fit a working lock on the door and so I would often not shower fully, just having a quick strip wash early in the morning before the rest of the house was up and about. The fact that the house was like a morgue didn't encourage showering either! The ice on the inside of the windows and the ability to mimic a dragon, made one's clothes want to stay put! Shower's were a luxury left for my aunt's house where there was a large brass lock on the door, ensuring that unwanted guests could not intrude!

I didn't know how to say to anyone what was going on, but was desperate to share with someone, anyone how things were at home. I developed a good relationship in Year 7 with my form teacher, who seemed to sense that all may not be as it seemed with me.

When asked, I stayed mute and covered for both my stepmother and father saying that I was happy, but that I missed my mum. I feel that back in the 80's there was less talk of safeguarding and teachers using their intuition in schools to make referrals to appropriate services to keep kids like me safe, and that had it been in the here and now things may have been different.

So, I minimised the emotional, physical and sexual abuse and did not ever see the potential for the abuse to escalate. I knew that most of my friend's did not have the same issues that I had and didn't dare share with them the actualities of my abuse, preferring to share with them how horrible my stepmother was to me.

I know that minimising and denying to oneself what has and is going on is typical of abuse victims. I wasn't being beaten or raped and so told myself to live with it! I had become so institutionalised by it and knew that I was virtually powerless to change things at that point.

My father, wanting to control me fully banned all boys from our house, even though I was great friends with both sexes and he banned me from wearing makeup to stop any male attention. I was blossoming into a pretty little thing and had started to get some attention from boys at school. My dowdy clothes, lack of make up and a trendy hair cut meant I felt unconfident and I knew that I was already tarnished goods.

My aunt, ever watchful as I grew up, noticed him wanting to keep me younger than I was and overruled him by buying me trendier, shorter clothes and shoes. He hated it, but I know that he was never going to 'fess' up his reasons for keeping me caged. She overruled the 'sensible school shoes and uber long skirt, that was three sizes too big and bought me a gorgeous flarey circular skirt that I twirled round and around in.

I spent more and more time at my aunt's as it was on my school route. I called in before and after school and stayed every weekend. I surreptitiously moved a few possessions into the spare room that I had claimed as my own and began to plot to leave the house.

Chapter 16 Hate

My relationship with my stepmother had deteriorated to the extent where she refused to cook for me or do my washing by the time I was around ten. Diligently, on a Friday night I would wash my uniform and get it ready for school on Monday. Our washing machine was in an outside shed and I frequently cried as I loaded my clothes into it, in the cold shed feeling a little like Cinderella, minus the fairy godmother!

I would then make my own supper from the items that I was allowed to use. The nice food, chocolate biscuits, crisps, fruit and cake which she had bought were strictly out of bounds. I remember trying to work out how many cherries I could take from the bag in the fridge before she noticed that they were gone!

This subversive behaviour reinforced her view of me that I was sly! If ever I was caught with contra-band food from her stash there would be hell to pay, with screaming and shouting, name calling and histrionics.

My father, ever the spineless idiot never challenged my stepmother about her behaviour and I just accepted that this was the way it was! All I wanted at that moment was for someone to champion me and stand up for what was so very wrong. I hold a small amount of gratitude for her in doing this, whilst it was not done to teach a life lesson, it certainly served as one, given that I quickly became highly organised and self sufficient and have become very passionate about being the one to stand up to the bullying and subjugation of others. Bullying makes me livid and I have no time for it.

Where ever possible I planned my escape and counted down the days until I could leave the house. Whereas most kids perhaps don't count the days down until they can leave home for good, I did. Days turned to weeks, weeks to months and month to years. I have learnt that time passes regardless of one's situation and that digging in and pre-occupying ones-self is a better strategy to moping around.

Most years I spent maybe a week in the summer with my mother in South Wales, at the house of fun and remember those times with fondness and joy. I never went at any other time strangely and I didn't see her on weekends.

Although it always felt like a holiday and that I was a guest, I used to dread being taken back, I remember it as a happy time. I would often sob all the way back and ask my mum to keep me down there with her.

We apparently had a conversation when I was around eight where she asked me if I wanted to live with her and I refused. It is not something that I have memory of, and I guess that at eight, most kids are not able to make such an important choice. I was told from an early age that the place where my mother lived was a drug den, filled with hippies and with frequent drug raids!

To a child who was fearful of the police and hated a lack of routine maybe these may have been the fundamental reasons for a refusal. I guess we will never know how things would have played out had I gone to live with my mother, aged eight. One thing is for sure, and that is, had I not endured what I endured then, I would not be me! I have learnt not to think about the what if's in life. I consider them a waste of time, effort and imagination.

When I came back from visiting my mother, my stepmother would ridicule my mother and make continuous comments about where she lived. I was told that I came back from her house filthy dirty, unwashed, riddled with worms and that my clothes were disgusting because my mother lived in such a pit. It was hard going, yet I noticed that my stepmother was never quite brave enough to say these things in front of my mother when she dropped me home.

There was much groveling and schmoozing from my stepmother towards my mum. Cups of tea were made, and polite chit chat ensued as my stepmother played super mum, pretending to dote on me! She even went so far to give me a hug and say she'd missed me! She deserved an Oscar Award, because as soon as my mother was safely off down the road the ridicule and bitching would restart.

I know that if at any time I had said anything to my mum about the way that I was being treated, that she, like others would have intervened and would have probably put my stepmother through a wall with her hands at her throat! Fearful of the consequences and petrified the nothing would change even if I told my mum about my home life, I just dug in and continued counting the days until I could leave!

Time passed by and I began to look forward to leaving junior school for pastures new. After an appeal, I had made it to the local Comp where lots of my friends were going. It was in a good area and had been developed on a new site.

I was excited for change and knew that leaving the security of my small school would mean that I would grow in confidence. It also meant that I could pop into my aunt's house every day, giving me respite from my stepmother, as it was legitimately on the way home!

Summer uniform shopping was traumatic that summer. I wanted to not look babyish, yet my father was determined to keep my looking like a five year-old. He refused to buy me a bra, for my budding breasts and insisted on knee high socks, sensible shoes and a revolting pleated skirt which hit my knees. My games skirt was below the knee and bizarrely still fitted me at twenty-five!

I hated everything, especially the black leather Polyvelt shoes! Revolting, clumsy black shoes with laces and a thick, sturdy sole which my father loved. I knew that I would be the laughing stock in the school and sobbed hysterically as the shopping trip progressed. Of course, I now realise that my father wanted to keep me young looking for his own perverted fantasies, but as an eleven-year old I only cared about fitting in.

Bless my aunt and nan. Ever my saviours I was whisked into town on the Saturday before school went back and bought white ankle socks, black slip on shoes and a lovely pleated short skirt.

The plan was to hide them at my aunt's house. I would call in there on my way to school and make a quick change before walking up the hill to school. On the way home, I would do the same thing and my father would be none the wiser! How smug did I feel, skipping to school in my ankle socks, a far cry from the knitted navy knee highs I was meant to be wearing!

All went swimmingly until early one morning my father drove past me as I walked to school in my contraband uniform and stopped the car. I was luckily with two friends, so he was forced to be nice, yet I could see him livid with anger as he told me that he would 'see me after school!'

I knew exactly what that meant and later after school I didn't bother going back to my aunts to change, choosing take my punishment of a smacked arse in the garage.

He didn't scare me one bit. I have to say that not a lot scared me, which in retrospect was peculiar in itself! I knew that I was in for a hiding and that day, feeling brave, I entered the garage with fire in my heart and courage in my belly. I did not, and would not back down.

My father loved to hold me by the arm as he went to strike me. It allowed him to grip me tight as he tried to smack my butt. I realise now of course that there was probably a sexual motive for his need to spank me, but in my naivety, I just knew that it hurt and that most kids my age were not hit and punished like this.

That day, as I sobbed silently with the unjustness of my situation I refused to be hit anymore. As he rose his hand I ran around him sniggering in delight. His hand came loose and he grabbed for me again. Around and around we went, him crazy with anger and me wetting myself with delight.

I was lightening quick as he grabbed for me again and again, furious over the lack of control. I guess he could feel his power over me slipping away and he was livid, and I guess scared about me revealing his past sins.

He finally managed to grab me by both shoulders and spinning me round to face him, dug his fingers into my scrawny shoulders. His words were like water off a duck's back to me then, as they are now, yet, I still remember them now.

'You are not looking like a slut, do you understand me?' He ranted.

I kept my council, looked him straight in the eye knowing that I had won and feeling totally empowered. What he didn't know at that point was that I had left the revolting clothes at my aunt's and would refuse to bring them back to the house knowing that my aunt would not let my father in the house to retrieve them. It was game, set and match for me and I realised that I was able to fight back.

Chapter 17 Running away

My father, as afore told, was a dreadful womaniser. He became charming and divine when he needed to and it was like watching a totally different man exude charm as he tried his luck with a friend of my godmother at a wedding. He would flirt with women in shops, at the leisure centre and women seemed to be attracted to him like flies around the proverbial turd!

At the wedding of his friend he was on top form, animatedly being vivacious and charismatic and I knew that he was smitten with the chief bridesmaid. I was a bridesmaid, which allowed me to stay up late and literally be party to the partying.

She was a far cry from the sour faced creature in my house. As an adult writing this I know that my stepmother was mortally miserable living with the abuse, violence and affairs, yet I alone know that everyone has a choice in their situation. For whatever reason my stepmother chose to stay, along with my siblings in an intolerable situation, and refused to change it. Perhaps she did not know how to change things or was scared of the repercussions. I doubt I will ever know what made her remain in such misery, yet I know that in watching her miserable existence it made me commit to a philosophy of ' if you don't like it change it'.

As a child I was unable to read the disquiet in their relationship and did not acknowledge that she should have and could have left the relationship, all I saw was a woman who hated me and was hideous beyond belief to me. I needed a new mum and saw the gorgeous chief bridesmaid as her.

I watched from a distance as they flirted and danced and became excited as they chatted. I was virtually planning their wedding! On the way home and in the days preceding the wedding I noticed a change in my father, from sullen and unhappy to excitable and playful.

I actively encourage my father to see her again and begged to be allowed to go with him to her house. He took along gifts and I remember that I watched TV as they went to another room. She had a lovely house and again, in my desperation to change my miserable existence in the small terraced house that was my virtual prison, I dreamed of living in this warm and cosy abode.

We drove home late and as he asked me if I liked her, I felt certain that he would marry this friendly, smiley woman. He made an excuse to see her on many nights, often using the sports centre and squash matches as an excuse to visit. I remember being dragged around the town looking for the right Christmas present for her, which was ironic as I rarely got a present from him!

I am not sure to be honest how my stepmother came to the conclusion that my father was having an affair, but one chilly afternoon I arrived home from school with the usual feeling of dread and anxiety which hit my stomach as I entered the road. I wondered what I may be blamed for, or called, or what chores I could be asked to do. Outside of the house I felt free and alive. Inside I felt sad and despondent.

Entering the front door, I sensed the atmosphere immediately. My heightened perceptiveness paid me dividends at an early age and I realised that my stepmother was waiting for me on the sofa. I tried to sneak past her, but in a 10ft x 10ft living room, there was nowhere to hide!

'Where did your dad go last night?' She asked, rising to her feet to stand over me. I took a sharp intake of breath and put down my school bag. How on earth a child should ever be put in this situation is frankly beyond me, yet I know now that it showed a blatant disregard for my wellbeing from my father.

'I don't know' I muttered, refusing to make eye contact.

Rough hands seized my shoulders and she dug her fingers in roughly.

'I know that you know her. Where was he? She hissed, fingers and nails pinching like tweezers as her grip tightened.

I fought back tears. Should I tell her, should I remain loyal?

'It's the woman from the wedding, I don't know her name' I blagged.

Accusingly she looked me in the eye. She was not upset, just angry. There seemed to be little jealousy, just anger that I knew what he had been doing and she clearly didn't.

I went to sit down on the sofa as she relaxed her grip and with relative eased moved around her in a full circle until I was behind her and near the front door.

She looked surprised as I wrenched open the lock and threw myself out onto the street into the chilly early evening air.

As I bounded down the path she came after me, yet I was fast. On a mission to escape. I was not going back. This was it, I was going to be free once and for all. She had no real desire to chase me. Once she realised that she couldn't catch up she vanished back into the house without a care in the world that she had watched an eleven-year-old child run away from home in a clear state of distress. I knew once again that my feelings did not matter and that I was not welcome nor safe in the house.

Running fast I ventured down to the park. For anyone who has ever run away from home you will know that ordinarily you get to the end of the road and have an over whelming compunction to return back home. Not this eleven-year old.

Despite being petrified for being so disobedient, terrified of the repercussions from my angry and volatile father and scared stiff of being abducted off the street by a murderous stranger I headed for my aunts' house. The one place that I felt safe. This was the second time that I had disobeyed my 'parents' and I was starting to like the thrill!

Even today my older children joke that I have a problem accepting authority! Ironic, given that I cry if I am pulled over by the police, yet authority that is without penalty I am happy to flout and openly disregard!!

By the time I had made it through the back gate into the garden I was soaked through. I had hoped that my aunt may have been home, but sadly the familiar glow of the kitchen light was out and the back door firmly locked.

The scary outside shed was locked, as was the wood shed. I was grateful for this on one hand given that it harbored some of the largest and fairest spiders known to man! My aunt would always quote the 80's film, or advert, screwing up her face saying 'there's something nasty in the wood shed'! I totally agreed and avoided the small, damp space like the plague.

The only dry place, shy of returning back to the hell house, which was never going to be an option was the garden swing. My aunt had a beautiful fabric covered garden sofa swing, that was her pride and joy. I would spend hours sat gently swaying on it, reading my books and now it became home.

I slid the waterproof cover up slightly and slipped under it, the cushions were damp and cold, but thankfully it was dry. I hugged my knees to my chest and finally let the tears flow. I didn't understand why things should be so bad and horrible for me. Why could no-one make the enduring hell stop? I knew the answer but knew that even if I confided in someone about the truth of living in the house there was a chance that nothing would be done and my confessions may just land me in even more trouble!

This was not a chance I could take. I sat and sang quietly to myself, picked my fingers and wished myself warm! It was beginning to get dark and I wondered at what point someone may just realise that I was missing. I was sure my stepmother was glad to see the back of me but hoped that she had let someone who cared for me know that I was upset and had run away.

I heard the back gate at that moment click open and heard the familiar squeak of trainers on the wet stone. I sat stock still, frozen and not breathing as my father stood in the garden jut a foot away from my hiding place. My heart beat a fast-paced rhythm in my chest and I felt like I was breathing so loud that my breaths could be heard miles away.

Satisfied that I was not in the garden, after what seemed like an eternity, he turned on his heel, farted loudly as he walked away and closed the gate with a click. I was free! I was freezing, starving and in desperate need for a pee, but I was free! I was not going back to that house ever! I would live under the canopy like a stowaway until I was old enough to make my own way in the world and be un-reliant on any grown up!

Of course, my plan failed! Less than two hours later I was rumbled by my nan who came to look for me in the garden. I cried into her warm shoulder and told her in broken sentences what had happened. I begged to not go home, but my words fell on deaf ears as my father drove to the house to collect me and return me back.

The atmosphere went from bad to worse and my relationship with both my father and stepmother degenerated. My father blamed me for my stepmother finding out about his illicit affair and my stepmother blamed me for just existing! The rows continued, the long silences and bitter quips were common place and my determination to get the hell out of dodge became more fueled with every passing day.

Chapter 18 Escalation

As I got older I spent more and more time at my aunt's. Going home filled me with dread and I felt sick and so sad as I entered the morose atmosphere in the building. The nit picking, and insults would start as soon as I entered a room and as I matured I found it increasing difficult to not answer back. The unfairness of being hated for no other reason, than her jealousy and her unhappiness drove me mad.

Over a relatively short period of time I began to answer her back and stand my ground. Unsurprisingly, she hated this, and it seemed to goad her more, but for me it was liberating. One evening there was an unprovoked, verbal assault on me over my apparent laziness and rudeness. Standing my ground and giving as good as I got at thirteen did not go well, and the personal insults about my mum and my own character flaws began in earnest.

Battle lines were drawn and in my desperation to shut her up I recall I uttered the words:

'Fuck Off'

You could have heard a pin drop as time froze and she slowly comprehended what had been said.

Seizing the moment to leave the room I took a chance and haired it up the steep Victorian staircase like a thing possessed, fell into my bedroom and shutting the door hard threw myself against the back of it. I knew I had crossed a line and that I would reap the consequences. I heard her storming up the stairs and was then torn between barring the door with my weight and throwing myself out of the first-floor window. The window idea won easily as I knew that my slight frame would not be able to hold off her adult bulk for long.

As she entered through the door, full of venom I was half leaning out of the window, back to the opening, working out the best way to lower myself down to the ground.

She crossed the room and grabbed me by the shoulders hard. She began pushing her weight towards me and I grabbed onto the window sill and frame to hold on.

'You little bitch' she snarled.

'You're pushing me out, I am going to fall' I sobbed, hysterical by now and fearful that in her rage she would tip me, back first out of the window onto the garden. It was in-fact around a fifteen foot drop and I knew that landing back first would injure or even kill me.

I had no leverage on the sill and moved further towards the aperture as she pushed harder. The red mist was down and she was at the point of no return.

'I am going to fall,' I shrieked again. My heart was beating out of my chest and I struggled to try and rationalise with her, words coming out shaky and broken.

'I will die if I fall, please stop' I begged.

At that very moment when I thought that I would be over the sill, a couple walked up the road. They stood stock still outside our house trying to comprehend what they were seeing.

'Oi' shouted the man. 'Everything all right up there?' He asked.

Without speaking she took her hands from my shoulders and saying nothing stalked back out of the room and down the stairs.

I wriggled myself off of the frame and slid down the wall, shaking like a leaf. She had tried to kill me. She had wanted to. She hated me so much I cogitated in my mind. I knew that I was not going to be able to stay in the house much longer and that in the interim I needed get out.

My father was out and it was the days before mobile phones. I felt stranded and totally alone. Phoning my mother was useless. She was three hour's drive away. And besides, I couldn't go and live with her. My aunt did not know much of what was going on and I didn't want to involve the parents of friends. I plumped for calling my grandparents but had to wait another thirty minutes for her to pack my sibling in the car and drive away. I had no idea where she was going, but knew that I needed to call for help NOW.

Scuttling down the stairs I rubbed my bruised shoulders and ran across the red tiled kitchen and picked up the phone. My softly spoken nan answered, and I felt my knees buckle and chest start to heave as I began to cry. In a broken, nonsensical fashion I tried to tell my nan that I had nearly fallen out of the window and had been pushed by my stepmother. I pleaded with her to ask my grandfather to drive over and collect me very soon, telling her that I was frightened and couldn't stay in the house.

Not really getting to grips with the severity of the incident she told me that grandad would be there in half an hour and to pack a few things. I filled a carrier bag with my precious things, not useful things but things precious to me and watched out of the window for my grandad's car. In the serendipitous manner that often occurs as my grandfather's familiar car came slowly up the road, my stepmother's car came into view behind it. You couldn't write this. Looking back, it resembled some poorly scripted episode of an afternoon soap!

My grandad got out of the car in front of the house and my stepmother parked behind him. With the safety of the car looming I was down the stairs, laden down with my chattels in a second and fell out of the front door into my grandfather's arms.

'Go and get in the car with nan Dand' he calmly told me.

Turning to my stepmother in a cold voice he said 'I know what's happened, Dand called us at home hysterical. I am going to take Dand back to ours. I do not want this to happen again.'

He turned on his heel and got back in the car while my stepmother stood gob smacked that I had called for help and had told another adult about her behaviour.

I remember that my grandmother never forgot that night. She carried it to her grave, only speaking of it when my brother, with whom I was close, asked her if it was true that his mother had treated me badly as a child. My nan told me that she had told him in no uncertain terms that my childhood had been less than ideal and that his mother was partly responsible. He seemed to believe her, and although we never spoke about it directly, we maintained a close relationship until my father's sins were uncovered.

My grandfather took me back to their familiar house and made me a snack. I was shaken and crying spasmodically and couldn't bring myself to re-live the incident fully to my nan. She saw how shaken I was and they both agreed that I could stay at their house that night. I went to bed in my nan's double bed feeling loved and secure. Sadly, it would be a while longer before this feeling was a regular occurrence in my life.

The following day my grandfather drove me back to my aunt's house at my request. While they talked over a cup of tea I went upstairs to the spare room. It had been known as the sewing room for obvious reasons, and had a chest of drawers, small built in wardrobe and single bed. It was at the top of the stairs and I loved it. It was peaceful, and the bed was warm and cosy. More-over it was in an environment where I felt safe and more loved.

Armed with my carrier bags I began to pop my stash of items taken from my bedroom into the drawers. I was careful to put them in the bottom draw and top wardrobe cupboard. I didn't want anyone to cotton on just yet that I had come up with a cunning plan.

Over the next few months when I came to my aunt's house on the weekends, I was going to bring my possession's bit by bit, so that neither household noticed too much. When the bedroom at my dad's house was empty of my things, I would ask my aunt if I could stay with her for good and never, ever go back to the house.

Chapter 19 The Last Straw

After a calmer weekend at my aunt's and armed with my plan I had to go back home. I had been reassured by my aunt that all was well and that there would be no repercussions or fall out from my stepmother. She was quieter than normal around me and the sniping stopped for a few weeks.

I think in all honesty she had shocked herself and was worried that she may get into trouble. I got on with making my own food and doing my own washing and using every excuse to spend as much time as possible to pop into my aunt's house, armed with more bits and bobs to be stashed in the 'sewing room', aka my new bedroom.

No-one had any reasons to go through the drawers or into the wardrobe and so no-one was any the wiser. I moved clothes, books and toiletries slowly to their new hiding place, feeling like the end to my nightmare life may be around the corner. Over the next month things started to get back to normal and the bullying began again.

One evening, shortly after I had turned thirteen, I was sat watching TV in the tiny living room. I was sat on the chair by the door minding my own business. My stepmother had ordered a new suite and it was a damn site more comfy than the wooden sided one that we used to have. As usual, as I still do, I was sat with my feet tucked up underneath me enjoying the peace and quiet.

My stepmother came in from work at around nine thirty and immediately stood behind the new chair scowling. My hackles rose as I knew that things were going to kick off and I felt myself tense for battle.

'Get off that chair' she spat. 'I bought it and you have no right to sit on it'

I didn't turn around to respond but ignored her and stayed stock still.

'I'm talking to you' she continued, raising her voice.

Again, I tried not to respond, knowing that anything that I said would inflame the situation.

She moved around the front of the chair and blocked my view, standing over me.

Still I played dead, choosing to look around her at the program. This tipped her over the edge and she flashed.

'I bought that chair and you will not sit on it, you will sit on the floor, now move' she screamed into my face.

She lent down and grabbed my arms roughly trying to drag me off the chair and onto the floor where I clearly belonged. I dug in and became a dead weight. She pulled harder and began to manhandle me off the chair. As my feet hit the floor I stood up and grabbed her shoulders too. We pushed and shoved as she tried to move me around away from her precious chair as I fought to stay put. I was not going to back down any more. The shy, bullied little thing was having no more of this bullshit.

She screamed obscenities at me and I hurried them back with venom, no holds barred. For all the times she had ridiculed, bullied and hurt me, I was a girl on a mission to retaliate. The damn had finally well and truly ruptured, and the situation had got fully out of hand.

She slapped me, a stinging blow to my cheek. I felt no pain, only more anger, and I raised my fist to hit her. I had no idea where my rage at her had come from, but I wanted blood. Yet, that tiny voice inside me told me to not hit her, but allow her to push me onto the floor, to hurt me as it would give me license to finally leave.

And that is what I did. I buckled my knees and came away from the chair. I dropped my hands and allowed her to shake me towards the floor. I said not another word. I didn't need to. I had won.

She had given me the perfect excuse to never be in that house again after that night. I was fearful that if I stayed either I would be seriously hurt or that I would be forced to hurt her in order to protect myself. I found myself thinking as an adult and not as the vulnerable child that I was.

Chapter 20 Leaving

The following morning still shaken, but jubilant I left for school with my bags a little heavier and my heart a lot lighter. I was armed with what looked like bags and kit for school yet was actually in the final stage of moving out completely. I was resolute in the fact that I would never be spending another night in the hell hole as long as I lived. I proudly nursed my battle scars and although there was no mark, whenever I touched my bruised cheek it reminded me that I was leaving.

On the way to school I dropped into see my nan. My aunt had gone to work early, and I ran past my nan to drop the final things into my newly claimed bedroom. I explained to my nan that I needed to stay in the house and that I couldn't go home. In some detail I explained to my nan about the fight and that I was scared for my safety. My nan, although shocked, reassured me that there would always be room in the five bedroom house for me. Little did she know that most of my things lay hidden in the 'sewing room' ready for when this day came.

I begged my nan to speak to my dad and tell him that for the time being I would be staying with her and my aunt while things calmed. This euphemism for 'she ain't never coming home' made my life easier, as my father foolishly was duped into thinking this was a temporary measure. My father agreed, that for the sake of keeping the peace I could stay on a temporary basis. I knew that once he realised that I was NEVER returning that he would know he had lost control and all hell would break loose.

For the next two weeks I lived an idyllic existence in my aunt's house. Warm towels, heating, a soft, safe bed and a lock on the door made me relax and recuperate. Having no-one to snipe at me was good for my confidence, yet in the back of my mind I knew that my father would be around soon to get me back.

Sure enough a few days later there was a buzz on the door bell. My aunt answered and I heard her greet my father.

'I've come to get Dani' he said grimly. 'I want her home'

My aunt invited him into the kitchen, in a formal fashion and I lurked on the upstairs landing, out of sight but able to hear everything. I knew that my aunt could handle herself and was not remotely afraid of my father. Her tone in addressing left me in no uncertain doubt that she had made her mind up that I was not going back.

For once having someone to fight my corner was liberating, yet I found myself crying at the confrontation that I could hear unfolding downstairs.

'I have told you that she is coming home and that this is not your decision at all,' my father said with a raised voice.

'And I have told you that she is not coming home. She doesn't feel safe and you don't protect her one bit' my aunt retorted.

'If she stays, I won't pay a penny towards her' my father came back vindictively, thinking that my aunt would immediately say, that for that very reason I could not stay. Thankfully she was not interested in the least in the money and it was a moot point. She probably will never realise the impact of her selfless decision. Many others would have shied away at being responsible for another child, financially and emotionally, yet she rose to the challenge, knowing there was no financial support from either my mother or father.

With that my father realised that he was on a hiding to nothing and flounced off out of the kitchen, stomped down the hall and left the house, slamming the large front door with a bang. I threw myself downstairs with joy and ran into the kitchen. I couldn't' believe it that I was now living here and there was nothing that my father could do.

As a mother who has brought up another woman's children with no financial support I truly comprehended just what my aunt did for me that day. She agreed that I could stay with her, without any monetary contribution from my mother or father because she loved me.

I felt indebted to her and set out being the best teenager ever. I did exactly as I was told, never back chatted, helped clean and tidy, never smoked, drank nor stayed out late in order to never give her an excuse to throw me out.

She called me boring and a goody two shoes when we laughed about it years later and although I agreed entirely that I was a boringly good kid, I explained to her my reasoning behind my behaviour.

The most daring and rebellious thing that I ever did was around the age of fifteen I put my watch back by an hour in order that I could stay out an hour later with a new boyfriend! My aunt nearly peed herself when I told her why I was late! 'Don't you think I tried that one too,' she laughed!! I was sprung and laughed back, immediately confessing my crime.

I think it made her glad when I behaved a bit more like a normal teenager to be honest, but I couldn't pretend to be something I was not. I was not going to rock the boat by doing anything to jeopardise my safe and happy new home.

Chapter 21 Happy

My teenage years at my aunt's house were some of the happiest of my life. She was kind, happy and treated me with respect and not like a small child. We had a more sisterly relationship and would sit chatting about all manner of 'stuff' when she was in the bath. No topic was off limits and I learnt all about relationships, sex and contraception through our frank discussions.

I was allowed friends over and they loved coming to stay. We sang, danced and roller skated up the long red tiled hall, cooked in the sage green kitchen and ran amok. I performed well at school and was often described as quiet, polite and hard working. I studied hard and was well liked by teachers and friends and can actually say that I loved school. It gave me routine and made me even more self motivated.

Very few people knew that I had run away from home and absolutely no-one knew that I had been abused in all manner of ways. I put this down my inner resilience. The ability that I have had from a young age to bounce back, see the positive and move forward with what was good in my life.

I went to my father's house as little as possible and stayed in the safe confines of my aunts lovely home. From the sewing room, which had been my sneaky sanctuary when I was stashing my possessions I moved to the larger back bedroom. This for me was a sign that I was a permanent member of the household and meant so much to me. I was no longer in the spare room, but had a gorgeous, safe room.

At fifteen I began a steady relationship with a fellow school mate. It was my first experience of love and I craved security. We talked of getting married and settling down. My aunt and my mum were horrified, given their teenage antics, which they had regaled me with on many an occasion. Yet, all I wanted was to be happy and content. I had no desire to shag my way around the school, drink, take drugs and experiment!

Boring yes, sensible absolutely!! You are reading the writings of a person who can hand on her heart say that she's NEVER, EVER tried a drug! Never taken a drag on a cigarette, and has only slept with five people!! I am the epitome of boring!!

Through hard work and dedication I did well in my GCSE's which allowed me to go on to study A-Levels. I was still clueless about jobs, but felt that I needed something sensible! I now know that this was more to do with wanting security and needing to be self sufficient. I was told at school that I had a fantastic voice and could act and dance.

Mrs P, my dance teacher tried in vain to get me to consider applying to Musical Theatre College. Yet this was an industry that I saw as being unstable, unreliable and precarious financially, thus I began looking at teaching and nursing. I felt that I needed stability and both paid well and would allow me to leave my aunts house to step out into the big wide world!

Two long years later I walked away from college. I had discovered cider and black, night clubs, dancing, midwifery and confidence. Despite flunking my A Levels with a terrible DD I had secured a place on a midwifery course based in Birmingham, starting in October 1992. I was so excited. I was to get paid £365 per month, was to live in nursing accommodation and would have a sought after profession which would keep me solvent.

All those years of waiting and counting down years before I could really stand on my own two feet and be a 'grown up' had come at last. I was sad to leave my aunt's house. She reassured me that I would always have a room in her house and that I would always be welcome. I love her dearly for this. Knowing that I had a home to come back to gave me that warm, safe feeling that I craved for so long.

The girl was finally a grown up!

Chapter 22 Dreams

As an adult, my dreams are that of a mad person. In bright technicolour, my mind tries to make sense of where I have got to with the relationships with people that I share blood with, yet do not call family.

In my dreams, I find myself in the garden of my mother's house. I have no idea how, or why I have gone there. The tiered garden looks down onto the corrugated iron roof of the chalet. The sun streams into my eyes so that I cannot see into the windows, but I noticed that the stable door from many years ago is open.

Tensely, I began to walk towards the back door, down the steps, which have in reality been removed for around twenty years. The garden, today looks nothing like it does in my dream, and the relationships which twenty years ago meant so much, like the garden have changed beyond all recognition.

I edge towards the back door, and step over the thresh-hold, into the kitchen. The breakfast bar dividing the living space from the kitchen is still there, as is the wooden panelled wall, dividing the bedrooms from the lounge. The red carpet is threadbare, as it was when I was a child and the sliding door into the loo is still present. It's bizarre how intense the experience is of being back into the house, with the décor as it was all those years ago. I know that the house as it stands today is nothing like this, and wonder what my dream is trying to teach or show me, by transporting me back in time.

I hear footsteps on the wooden suspended floor and turn quickly to find my mother behind me. She touches my shoulders and I slowly turn around.

She is as I remember, attractive, ageless, with the bouncy black hair which I so craved as a child. She still carries weight, and this gives her a solid aspect to her frame. She is short, only five feet two-ish, and we stand eye to eye, given that I inherit my short stature from her.

She doesn't however take me into her arms and hug me like she used to. Like she used to back in the days before I challenged her and questioned how she treated me differently, before I got labelled as needy and prickly, back in the days when I thought I was mad, wrong and all things in between. Instead, she looks at me curiously and asks me,' what do you want'? I cannot answer or speak, it is as if my throat is closed over.

I always found it so difficult to tell her how I felt, how sad I felt, how lonely and left out I was and how different I felt. Yet in this nocturnal scenario I am even more mute, helpless, without a voice. Reverting back to the Dani, as I was before the shift, before the change, before the loneliness transcended over me like a hurricane and left me reeling into the darkness.

'You know how I feel about you' she says, looking me in the eye. Shameless, without emotion.

'You are difficult and demand so much of me, my time, my energy, my love' she continues, never taking those eyes, my eyes off of me.

I try to speak, to answer her back and tell her that I didn't mean to come, that I had lost my way and found myself there accidentally. I want to tell her that I had just been wanting to walk to the cliffs, the sea, the old castle ruin and Horse Shoe Bend.

Places which lie licked into my heart with their beauty but had got lost. Rationally I know this is an impossibility. I know that area like the back of my hand. The tracks, the bushes and the dunes. But, in my dream I cannot rationalise this and I remain wordless.

'I just don't love you like I love the others you know, not in the same way. You were always wanting so much of me, my time, my love. You had no idea what it was like for me, with you wanting so much, suffocating me with your neediness.' She continues.

And so, the assault continues. A replica of our last ever conversation when all became clear about the truth of her feelings, the differences she felt between me and my siblings. The revelation.

'You are prickly and difficult to be around, you know' she states, matter of fact, emphasising her words, as the tears fall silently down my face, rolling like a torrent. The tears fall for every word I cannot say back to her in response, yet still she does not yield or soften.

Her heart is dead to me, and I begin to feel suffocated, unable to draw breathe, my wordless mouth full of the things I wanted to say, but can't. I try to clasp my hands over my ears, to shut out the words which latch onto my soul, like black vultures, tearing me apart, but like my broken mouth they too are broken, heavy at my sides. I feel bile rising in my throat, the darkness rising up accompanied by vomit, wanting to empty myself onto the thin, red carpet, to exorcise those demonic words which hold me back.

Yet my mouth just won't open and I feel the warm bile and vomit began to track back down my windpipe, burning and stinging as its acidic consistency begins to score away at the fragile lining of my esophagus.

She watches as I struggle for breath, panicking and struggling. I can no longer hear her words, just see her mouth moving through the blurred tunnel of my tears. As I collapse to the floor, legs buckling under me I look at her one more time as I drown in the wrath of her words and the vomit.

I wake up sobbing uncontrolledly, gasping for the breath that I couldn't find in my dream. My limbs are rigid and fixed, hands clasped into fists with my nails digging into the palms, transferring the pain from my heart into a real sensation. I am soaked in sweat and my mind is racing. The words were real and have all been spoken out loud before, yet still have the caustic effect on me as when they were first uttered.

These dreams have become part of my being since I made the decision to change three years ago, aged forty-one. That day when I finally came to realise just why I was the odd one out and why I felt so different.

Chapter 23 Heaven Gains Another Star.

My Nanny W was my idol. She was gentle and kind, loved me unconditionally and spoiled me rotten. I believe from anecdotal tales passed down from my mum and aunt that she was not always this maternal and nurturing. She had endured hardship and was married three times, which for a woman of her age was a little 'Liz Taylor-ish'

She had married her childhood sweet heart. They shared a birthday and went to the same school and were neighbours. She loved him with all of her heart, and I believe she never stopped loving him.

They married during the war and he was sent back to his deployment. With tragedy, of Shakesperian tales he was killed when his plane crashed on the way back from Burma, just after the ending of the war. After that she had a second failed marriage that ended in divorce and promptly took herself off to Australia on a boat to live for a number of years.

What a strong and feisty young woman she was. I think that the females in our family have such a lot to be thankful for with such a strong and dynamic role model in her.

When she returned she was introduced to my grandfather, Edward. He was an older business man who was besotted with her. She was beautiful, elegant and refused to do his bidding, resulting in violent and aggressive behaviour barraged towards my petite nan. She would not be taken down lightly and I am told that she gave as good as she got.

They birthed two daughters, my mum and my aunt. Both chalk and cheese, my mum, her dads favourite, because of her grit and feistiness and my aunt, who was my nan's favourite. She was delicate and less confrontational than her sister. Both girls grew up in a house with violence and angst.

My mother rebelled against her mother and my nan struggled to relate to her outlandish behaviour. When my mother married my dad, aged just eighteen, I would imagine that my nan was relieved to have had her daughter begin to finally conform to the norm.

When I was born in September 1973, six weeks premature, I believe that my nan was besotted with me. Between her and my aunt, they helped my mum with me, creating a deep bond between us. My nan bought me my first doll and first little Triang dolls house. The doll had black skin and jet black wavy hair. She was beautiful.

My nan hand knitted her a whole wardrobe of clothes in her neat stitch and I thought nothing when she named her 'chocolate'!! I obviously had no idea about the racist connotations of this name, and believe that back in the early seventies there were no barriers to stop such racist language. I still have the pretty doll with her hand knitted clothes in peach and yellow.

I spent many weekends with my nan and loved her with all of my heart. They say that when someone dies, that their voice is the last thing to fade in your memory. I can still hear her dulcet tones ringing in my ear as she answered the phone and as she gave me the hugest hug, telling me 'I love you, I love you, love you.'

As I became a mum myself my nan showed herself to be a devoted great grandma and relished time with the children. She was the most accepting of all my family when I told her that I had left my husband and met someone else, asking me 'are you happy?'. She seemed genuinely pleased when I told her that I was ecstatically happy with my choice.

I spent as much time as I could with her, but am guilty of pretending that she would always be there. I never considered that she might not be around for ever and that she was getting older and more fragile.

Before the ridiculous legalities of taking your children out of school in term time ensued, we took all six of our children down to the south of France for three weeks. It was relaxing and beautiful with many memories made and photographs taken.

Upon our return on Thursday afternoon I received a call from my aunt to say that my nan had been admitted to hospital with a chest infection. I had planned to go and visit her the next day, a Friday, as the house looked like a chinese laundry and I was knackered after a fifteen-hour drive back home. However, having sorted the kids out with supper and baths, I guilty admitted that I should go to see nan that evening.

In good spirits and sporting a tan and a bunch of flowers I made my way to the ward at the local hospital. It was a warm evening and still light. As I checked onto the ward I was shown to a side room where my nan slept. I quietly crept up to her and kissed her cheek and hand. She looked tired, and opened her eyes in recognition. 'hello darling' she said quietly.

I asked her if she wanted water and, finding the glass empty I wombled up the ward to find the kitchen or a member of staff. Quite at home on the ward, because of those many years spent on the ward as a midwife I came across a nurse and a doctor standing chatting in the corridor.

Politely I asked where the kitchen was and queried the whereabouts of my nan's menu for the following day's meals. Being A-tuned to body language, was impossible to miss the exchange of glances between the staff as they listened to my question. Resting her hand gently on my arm the nurse said, 'there's a quiet room over there, why don't you have a chat with Dr Jones?'

Sensing that all was not well, I took the Doctor's lead and followed him to said, quiet room. I knew that this did not bode well. Quiet rooms had only one purpose, which was to provide a quiet space in which to break bad news.

I couldn't have been more right. 'Take a seat, Mrs Downey' said the quietly spoken man. 'Do you know what is wrong with your grandmother?'

I explained how I had been to France for the past three weeks, and how this was first-visit to see her. Through eyes that began to well up I looked at him and knew that he was going to tell me that my beloved nan was dying, even before he had spoken those words. Intuition is a wonderful beast, but it sometimes means that you are a few seconds in front of a conversation or situation, and this results in the whole event slowing down, as if slowed by a magical entity.

'She's dying isn't she' I gasped, saying those words out loud.

'Yes. I am afraid that she is. She's in respiratory failure and there is nothing else we can do. She didn't want to be resuscitated and we wanted to let her go quietly. She hasn't got very long left, I am afraid. Is there anyone that you need to call?' he asked, with the quiet efficiency of a doctor.

Ignoring his question 'There must be something else that you can do, she spoke to me and knows that I'm there, she looks fine' speaking to him as if he was stupid!

'Her respiratory system has shut down and that will affect the rest of her body, we don't know how long this will take, but I am afraid that within the next day or so, she will pass away.'

It was around seven o'clock and with tears streaming down my face, I excused myself from the conversation, realising now that time was very short. I had only a few hours left with this very precious human being.

My aunt had popped off the ward to go home and whilst sat back at the bed side, listening to the gentle rasp of my nan's laboured breathing, I called my aunt. I was in total automaton making the call, calm, collected and forward thinking.

'I think you need to tell mum and anyone else who wants to get up to see her that they need to come NOW. They only have tonight. She's going' I told her.

'I'll phone them,' she said, 'and I'll be back as soon as I can, are you OK there by yourself?'

I told her that I was fine, but to hurry back.

I closed the door to the small white room and sat, stock still. I reached for nan's warm, thin hand and squeezed it gently. She squeezed it back and murmured.

She was propped up on pillows and I leant over her, wrapping my arms around her, as much as those bloody, bulky cushions would allow. I touched her cheek with my cheek and smelt the beautiful smell of her. The soft, grey hair, that had in her youth been titian red. Her blue, grey eyes flickered occasionally, giving me a view of those piercing blue irises, which had been passed down to my beautiful daughter. I felt her chest rise and fall as I cuddled her, and I know that she knew that I was there and could hear me as I softly sang to her.

Songs from my childhood, that I knew by heart, words cherished from the musicals that she had indoctrinated in me as I grew up. As a nurse popped her head through the door, I didn't let up with my singing. I knew that I was trying to sing life into her broken lungs, to help her mend and that it was futile, but still I sang. I held her hand and felt her squeeze it as she recognised the words from South Pacific, from the King and I and other such greats.

I thanked her for her love and told her that I loved her beyond belief, more than she could know, and I cried. A constant river of snot and salty tears streamed from my orifices. For anyone who has watched someone die before their very eyes, it's a helpless, hapless feeling. The grief is physical, raw and made me want to scream at the top of my voice at how unfair it was and how I wasn't ready for her to go. The small, functional and rationale part of my brain knew that it was futile and would only distress her more. I held onto this as my grief built up.

Around two hours later my mum and aunt arrived. My mother, clinical and unemotional at the impending death of her mother, and my aunt, feeling out of control in this alien environment, like a spare part, disbelieving that 'nanny' would be going so quickly. I held onto my aunt, knowing that she felt my pain, but would refuse to acknowledge or show it as readily as I was. My mother sought out the doctors and wanted to know exactly what was going on, as her breathing got more laboured and harsh. I knew that her time on this mortal plane was shortening by the second and that she was not much longer for this world. How, I thought, can someone be here at 7pm and gone by nearly 11pm? This wasn't in my plan!

As she began to become distressed and restless we spoke with a young doctor about giving her some drugs to calm her down. She was beginning to fight for breath, and it was hard to watch. Had she been an animal, they would have let her pass over, with dignity, hours ago.

We knew with absolute certainty that in giving her some drugs to settle her breathing, that there was a strong chance that it might bring on her passing a little quicker, and reduce the risk of her hanging on, struggling for breath for many hours. She was a stubborn woman in life, and it appeared that even in death she was the same. She would go when she was good and ready and not one moment before.

As the doctor prepared the drugs, I held her hands, and spoke to her about meeting Bob, her first husband again. 'Go and find him nan, he's waiting for you, can you see him?' I asked her.

She smiled, hearing what I was saying, and reacted with apparent joy. 'Can you see him, he's there in the light' I urged her forward, to leave the bodily pain and strife in this life, and move onto the next.

The young doctor, with the efficiency of one ingrained into the business of the NHS appeared, like Uncle Ben with a syringe of drugs. He was now the gate keeper, between life and death.

We asked for the priest to come and give her the last rites, rationalising that because she liked singing carols, at Christmas, she would appreciate this religious gesture! I am sure he thought we were mad! Laughing and joking with the priest in the corridor, before he went into the room to see her, for one last time, before the 'relaxing' drugs were administered.

I paced the corridor, like a wounded animal, as my mother, ever the epitome of calm and collected showed no emotion at all. My grief was palpable, touchable and my heart felt like it was being torn in two. My guardian angel, was so close to death.

Like the angel of death the doctor checked my nans details on her name band with the nurse and administered the drugs. I held her hand tightly, and gently placed my fingers on her pulse where no one could see. The drugs took no effect for a good few minutes, as I watched the clock, tick by on the wall. Her breathing seemed calmer, less laboured and she was taking longer breaths, less often.

Her pulse was strong and regular, as if fighting to stay alive, ignore the internal battles that were ensued in her body, as she struggled between the corridor of dark and light. In my mind, I saw her, ethereal like, walking slowly towards the light and beauty of a better place and I urged her on. Her respiration rate was slower now and her pulse under my fingers had noticeably slowed too. It was strong, but much more erratic, as if it was considering each and every beat.

She looked calm and peaceful as that final breath inhaled, then exhaled, and then nothing. Her heart beat made one thump under my fingers, then came a huge gap, as I waited for the next melodic beat, yet nothing. How the fuck can that be so? One minute beating, the next minute not so. It still messes with my head, even now.

She was gone and with it my angel and guardian. I kept my fingers on her wrist and her warm hand clasped in mine as I laid my head on the bed listening to the sound of my sobs, muffled by the clean white sheets. She looked finally at peace, and twenty years younger. My eyes played tricks on me, and I was sure that her chest was rising up and down, but sadly, her pulse confirmed that she had passed over to the land of eternal peace, to be reunited with those she had loved and craved for so long.

After a period of time the nurses tried to get us to leave the room. They wanted to lay her body out, and from being on the wards as a member of staff I knew that processes often took over at times like these. More than likely, there would be another person needing the bed within the hour, and although I sympathised with the NHS constraints I was reluctant to allow them to move her so soon. Press-ganged into moving from her bedside I kissed her on her wrinkle free forehead and left the room, feeling sick with grief.

Once again, ever the control freak I stopped myself from screaming out-loud to release the pain in my heart. I was stopped by the thoughts, that staff might think I was mad and that if I openly showed weakness, I might then be considered weak and vulnerable forever.

The moon was out as we stepped outside, and all I could do was gaze at the ether and wonder where she was and if she was looking down on me. I willed her to send me a sign that she remembered me or was present by me, yet none came. The mood was sombre, yet my mother seemed relived and unable to fathom the grief that I clearly displayed.

Once the body was laid out we went back to say our final goodbyes. I laid my head on my nans silent chest and wept once more at my loss and for the love I felt for her. Death is so peculiar, isn't it? One minute someone is alive, heart functioning and the next minute, the heart stops and all is silent. The mechanics of death surprised me, in the way that the heart suddenly ceased beating and that was it! For a midwife, I guess that you think I am quite stupid, but the finality of death still perplexes me.

As I sat outside the room, dazed and bereft I wrote this poem on a scrap of paper. It is my small reminder of the night I lost my angel.

Hard rasping breaths, labored, staccato

You Lie, unwakening.

Mind elsewhere, in happy times

I stroke your hand and struggle to maintain a calm face

Inside I scream and yell, ' Don't go please, I love you so'

The memories rush, torrential back to me

I try and capture them all, knowing that time is short

Not wanting to believe that by the moon's bedtime you will be a star eternal in the sky.

Your pulse plod's on, melodic, never bounding, sometimes pondering awhile over a beat.

Are you wondering, is it time yet?

I know you approach the white light, yet feel that every now and again you turn back towards me to wave and smile.

'I love you, love you, love you darling' you used to say.

As I weep at your shoulder and thank you for the wonderful times we shared

Your soft hugs and fond hugs, you move your hands in response.

I know you can hear me, but are further away now than ever.

Time speeds ahead and hour's turn to minutes.

As you linger at the bright light, your journey's end you become calm

and the mechanics begin to fail.

No repair can be done.

Your breathing slows and your pulse becomes hesitant

I wait,

Holding your hand, desperate for your the next breath

Yet it does not come.

You are but a memory laying in the bed

I imagine you gleefully meeting the many who have passed before you

I cry, tears so many as the grief surrounds me, engulfs me and eats me alive.

I love you, love you, love you with all of my heart.

Chapter 24 Life Goes On

We drove back to the house and bizarrely spent an hour sat in my living room, drinking tea, reminiscing about her. About her love of music, her penchant for sherry at Christmas, and about the time that she had beaten my mother over the head with a meat tin in rage, when she had an overactive thyroid!

We decided that my mother, ever the wind up probably deserved it! I recounted the time I had wound her up and she had tried to tip an open tin of baked beans onto my head! She was angry and so frustrated when she realised that it had cling film over the top of it!! Through tears, and with some silences we talked and laughed at our memories.

The following day life was back to normal for me. Kids woke up early and bounced around the house, the younger ones oblivious to my red eyes and constant crying. I sat the older ones down and told them gently that nanny W had been very sick and had become an angel, and that I was very upset and was crying because I was so sad. I wanted them to try and rationalise my grief and tears and felt it important to let them know that death happens to us all, that it is ok be sad and cry, and that it is not a form of weakness. They cried with me on that day, with Minner taking on a motherly role and cuddling me and asking me if I was ok, at every opportunity.

On a trip to Tesco's later that afternoon I found myself walking round the isles sobbing, unable to control the tears, much to the distress of the check-out lady.

Grief is hard, as is death. I had no idea that it would cause me a physical pain and although I knew the theory about the cycle of grief I found it hard to believe that I would move through the stages at all. It came suddenly, engulfing me, stopping me in my tracks at the slightest memory, small or thought. I still cannot listen to the song 'Run' which was in the charts, sung by Leona Lewis at the time she died. It talks of that goodbye and takes me back to the dark heart of grief all those years ago.

In planning her funeral my mum and aunt took charge. They cleared her flat, and I took bucket loads of things to the charity shop. Because her flat was owned by the council there were strict guidelines for the return of the keys, because there was another elderly person waiting to hot bunk in the bedroom!

I had always asked my nana for her gold tea set and was delighted to be given it by my aunt. As a tiny girl I had asked innocently 'nanny, when you die please can I have your golden teapot?'

In the hunt through nan's possessions they had found the telegram from the MOD sent at the time of her first husband's plane crashed, informing her that her was missing, presumed dead. It was a sad piece of paper, that had been kept for nearly seventy years, stashed away, through two other marriages and another long term relationship and was massively sentimental to my nan. I felt strongly that it should go in the coffin with her as it was hers to keep and not ours. There was a little resistance to this, but both sisters conceded eventually, that this was the right thing to do.

How strange is it that when we die our worldly goods are useless to us? All the material goods, the clutter, that we have collected and bought in our lifetime are worthless. What struck me at this point in time was the importance of the legacy that you leave behind and the effect that you had upon those whom you knew.

It makes me strongly want to leave a good, positive legacy when my time to go comes, one in which I had enhanced the lives of those who knew me and made the world a better place than when I found it. I guess this is my driver in writing this book. To show you that there can be good come from bad, light from darkness and courage over fear. If my story can help just one person take another step forward then my work is done.

This gave me a sense of purpose and helped me to see a positive aspect to such a sad time in my life. I tried to focus on the wonderful memories of my nan, of her kindness, her love, her strength, her satirical and often inappropriate sense of humour, and her wonderful voice, which has passed down through me and my children. I'm not saying that the loss ever leaves me, but I live with it nowadays, safe in the knowledge that I was loved and that my life is richer for knowing her.

Chapter 25 The Secret Unlocked

I was broken hearted at the funeral and took to running away for a few hours, refusing to answer my phone, wanting to be left in the vice like lock of my sorrow. I sat in the cemetery before the service chatting to my nan and when the time came for me to walk home I walked slowly, trying to delay the inevitable. It was a scorching hot day and I felt ridiculous in my funeral attire. It was a usual sombre affair and one which I felt exhausted at the end of it as a result of the emotion and sorrow that I felt. My mother tired to be empathetic, yet told me she was glad that nanny was dead, as she hated her. I felt like piggy in the middle.

The relationship with my mother at this point was about to reach a turning point with the fall-out from me revealing my darkest secrets, which I had kept close to my chest all those years would prove to be catastrophic.

Some weeks after the funeral, with the kids safely at school or nursery I spoke with my mother. I was telling her how sad I still was and how much I missed my nan. She retorted that she didn't miss her mum at all, in-fact, hated her and couldn't see why I was so devastated. This wasn't the first time that I had heard this, but on that day in particular, it hit a nerve.

In anger and without thinking of the repercussions I cast my die and blurted out 'Because, she was my angel, my saviour from the abuse. My dad sexually abused me. I cant remember exact details but I know that it happened.'

The line went quiet, the silence was awkward and charged and I could almost hear her mind whizzing around, hunting for clues and a rationality to clarify what I had just disclosed after nearly thirty-eight years.

'You still there'? I asked.

'I didn't know' she said, sounding shell shocked.

'I didn't tell anyone, you weren't to know' I soothed her, apologetically.

'Does Arty know, or did nanny'?

'No, no-one other than Charlie. It's not your fault' I continued.

'I'm going to kill him. Fucking, twisted, sick bastard !' she ranted, anger now seeming to engulf her.

'No, don't do that, it won't help, you steer clear.' I once again rationalised, feeling like the grown up.

I glanced at my watch, 'I've got to go mum, the kids need picking up, I'll speak to you later.' I said terminating the call and feeling like a weight had lifted off of my shoulders. The outcome from this point onwards was not the fairy tale ending that I had hoped for.

That evening the phone rang. It was my aunt. She appeared to be as shell-shocked as my mother.

'Why didn't you tell someone? We would have stopped it', she gently asked.

'I tried once, but they took no notice, I figured that it happened to every child, but I guess I was just unlucky, it happened to me with three different people.'

The conversation ambled on, with the general gist being that my aunt and mum were horrified and trying to work out why they hadn't known. I found it hard, as I had rationalised it years before and had mentally filed it away and had temporarily dealt with it. I must have seemed calm and untouched by the horror of my childhood. I had hoped that in revealing the abuse that it might unburden me a little and that secondly, it might help my mother understand me a bit more, and that this might in a bizarre way, help our relationship.

It was however my aunt who was happy and more comfortable with talking to me about the abuse and was much more open about it. My mother seemed unable to deal with it and given that we didn't see each other much, the relationship seemed to begin to change. My aunt, whom I saw much more often shared with me a little bit about my mother and father's relationship when they were together, and it was no surprise to me that he had physically and sexually abused her too.

I still find it outrageous that one person can commit such atrocities, which are hidden for many years because of the shame and silence associated with the abuse. These unspoken secrets increase the power that the abuser has, and make it more likely that they will get away with their crimes and commit these abhorrent crimes again.

If you are reading this I would encourage you to disclose your abuse to someone who you trust. It may be a teacher, friend, counsellor, help line or relative. The act of disclosing the abuse helps to break the power that the abuser has over you and begins to heal the wounds.

If you are an adult who is given a disclosure by a child, please remember that children don't make this kind of stuff up! It takes courage to tell someone about what is going on and if their disclosure is ignored or disbelieved then they may well never tell anyone again. We all want to be believed and to know that someone else is now involved and has our back.

I had hoped that my disclosure, inadvertently might make my mum love me more. How needy is that! As I write it I realise that it sounds so fucked up, but I am trying to be brutally honest with you. I now hoped that she would acknowledge that my childhood had been worse than horrible and that she would almost love me more to make up for leaving me in the hell hole of my world in the house. I had hoped that she would make up for lost time and begin to treat me like she treated my siblings. Sadly, my disclosure was to change the relationship with her, and my family catastrophically.

The sins of the fathers had ensured that the nuclear holocaust caused by the actions of one small and insignificant man would continue to have massive repercussions for me.

Chapter 26 Time Waits For No Man

My life moved on at speed. With the children growing rapidly and the gulf growing between myself and my mum with every conversation. Things were fine as long as we kept the relationship to a phone call, yet the moment that it demanded face to face contact, or a time commitment she seemed unable to commit.

One Sunday, I had invited my mum and step dad to our house for a Sunday roast. We had discussed them getting to us for around noon, ready to sit down for lunch at around 1pm. The kids were desperately excited about seeing their grand-parents and I was looking forward to having a few hours with my mum, in my house without the hub-bub that occurred in her home in Wales. I prepped and planned, baked and preened getting the meal just so. By 12.20 there was no sign of my guests, so I phoned their house phone. A sleepy, sounding voice answered the phone.

I knew immediately that they hadn't left, weren't even on their way and were actually still in bed. My heart fell, disbelieving that this could happen and feeling totally crushed for my children who were so looking forward to seeing her.

'You haven't left yet then?' I asked, not wanting to rock the boat.

'No, the band had a gig last night and we didn't get in until 4am. We'll get up and leave soon' was my answer.

I was in that familiar quandary. I wanted to vent and lash out with hurt, yet for some reason, known only to me, I felt unable to do it. I was confident and assertive in all other walks of life, yet with my mother I felt totally inept to voice my feelings and hurt. It was like I was back in child mode, not wanting to rock the boat, for fear of the consequences causing a catastrophic ship wreck, from which survival was unlikely.

'We were expecting you at 12, its 12.30 now, and it takes you two and a half hours to get here. You won't be here until at least 3pm, and lunch was planned for 1pm'. I tried my best to be firm, expecting a wealth of apologies and the like, but got none.

'We'll get up now and be with you in a bit' was my answer. She sounded pissed off, irritated almost that I had questioned this and was showing my annoyance.

'You have let me and the kids down' I blurted out, unsure where that came from, and immediately wishing that I hadn't said it. It was that classic SORRY, NOT SORRY moment. I knew that I had gone too far, and was too weak and insecure in myself to push this further.

'Don't worry about getting here now, we'll have lunch and go out, by the time you get here it will be time for you to go back home again'. I pulled back the situation, knowing that she was shocked that I had for the first time ever, called her out on her actions.

With tears running down my face I hung up. I felt like a naughty child who had been so bad that they couldn't be loved, yet logically I knew that I was right. She had been rude in not getting to the house on time, had been dismissive in the amount of hurt that she had caused and had attacked, when called out on her actions. That wasn't a balanced relationship, one with a foundation of love and respect, but at that moment in time I felt like I had pushed her away, and I knew that should I ever decide to challenge her in the future that I would regret the consequence.

I felt sorry for my rock of a husband in these situations. He could see the damage that the relationship did, and how distraught I was. He saw how needy I was for her to love me and have me as part of her life, yet chose his words carefully. Offering hugs and warm words, never openly slating her or her behaviour.

It would be many years before I changed the status quo.

I didn't hear from my mother for many weeks as a punishment for being difficult and not accepting the situation. It played on my mind and the more days that passed without a phone call the more I knew that I had royally upset her. Logically, I knew that I had a right to be upset, but I had such a skewed view of the situation, I couldn't see it clearly.

Chapter 27 Flash Backs

I had no time to sit and feel sorry for myself. The kids took up all of my time, and I worked as a midwife most of the weekends. If you have children you will know that life can be busy. I had six children under eight years old at one point and don't recall ever getting a moment to myself to breathe, yet alone pee! I was spread thinly and was constantly exhausted, yet kept on being mum to my brood, a wife to Charlie and all things to many other people.

My girls began to row on the river as they got older. It was a cheap pastime yet one which they enjoyed. They were both beginning to blossom into young women, wearing shorter skirts and midriff tops. It was about this time that I noticed my father looking them up and down. I kept contact to a minimum, and wouldn't let him be alone with the children, and his blatant response to the girls made me well aware that I was right about his motives.

As most survivors of abuse may testify, it was difficult to bring old issues up. My recollections of the actual abuse were hazy, and although I knew it had happened, I could not at that point say how it had happened. This left me in a position of uncertainty, wondering sometimes if I was crazy.

I had confided in my aunt and mum about it, yet still had moments of incredulity about the finer details. Your brain seeks to protect you so much I believe, and will only allow you to expose what it is you can cope with.

One Saturday morning, after rowing, my girls said that they'd seen my dad watching them row from the main bridge. Without prompting they both said that they found him creepy, and that they wouldn't feel comfortable being alone with him. This said so much to me. I had always taught them to use and trust their intuition, and yet, without any coaching or mention of my childhood experiences, they had come to this conclusion themselves.

It was time to move away, I decided on the spot. I wanted my children to feel comfortable and at ease in their house, and I knew that if we remained local there was more chances for my father to just drop round to the house. Without further ado, or time for contemplation, the house went on the market and six months later we moved fifteen miles away. Our new house was positively palatial, compared with the old, smaller bungalow, which was akin to the old woman, living in the shoe! It needed work, had only three bedrooms, yet we loved it. It was down a quiet cul de sac, with magnificent views of the valley.

My mother and aunt helped me to move, along with the six children, aged between, eleven and three! I was so grateful for their help in unpacking boxes and making up the six beds! My mother spent the day telling me how unsuitable the house was for the family, and how we were never going to make any money on it! For someone who had lived in a tin shack for most her life, and never renovated a property, I thought this was a bit rich, yet, once again, I kept my council. Ever fearful of being rejected or labelled difficult!

I saw great potential in the house and loved its security, its spiritual feel, being in the foot of the huge Malvern hills and I loved its space. It was far enough away from my father, for the children and I to feel more at ease.

I ignored my father's calls and requests to visit, yet embraced the chance to spend more time with my grandparents. They were able to drive over and come for Sunday lunch or cake. My nan loved the garden and would just sit and gaze out of the window at the view. As a keen gardener she was my go to person when I had questions about plants.

My version of gardening is to take a pair of loppers and cut things down! I am thankfully skilled in other areas, and now leave gardening to the professionals! Gardening aside, my nan and I had a beautiful relationship. We shared a mutually, inappropriate sense of humour and I think I replaced the relationship that she missed having with her daughter Anne.

Anne had moved away from the family home, at the earliest opportunity and came home to see her parents very infrequently. I found it hard to not feel animosity towards Anne, when I saw my nan so upset from time to time. I was desperate to be as loved by my mum as Anne was loved by my nan. I know this is reason that I felt such angst towards her.

I always made sure that if I drove to my nans home, that my father's car was nowhere to be seen. If he walked into the house while I was there, I by now, had the guts to walk straight back out again. I know that it perplexed and upset my grandparents, yet, what was the alternative? That I told them the truth or pretended that nothing was wrong? I was comfortable with neither option. I was determined that those sins of my father, would not impede another relationship.

Seasons passed, from Winter to Spring, and the children continued to grow. In amongst the chaos of our daily life with six kids, a job, a dog and a husband who worked away from home, Monday to Friday life passed by in a daze. I was on that proverbial hamster wheel of life and sometimes couldn't keep up! I worked weekends as a midwife and loved just going to work and not being called mum!

I know that being called mum is a privilege and that not all women can birth a child or adopt, but those precious few hours on a weekend spent as Dani, the Midwife meant so much. They gave me an identity outside the home and made me feel valued as a person. It was also important to me that I worked. I wanted to be a good role model to my children and allow them to see that there was little time in life for excuses.

Chapter 28 Stress

From 2007-2011 we spent many wasted hours in the family court system. My step children's mother, refusing to concede that she was vastly inadequate as a mother, and unable to put the needs of her two children before that of her own, took us back to the family court time and time again. In 2007 she had decided that the two small children had served their purpose in gaining her a larger percentage of a hefty divorce settlement, and having spent it she decided that she did not really want or need the two valuable commodities any longer.

I had my fourth baby in the February and in early May, having had no contact with the children for five months, she over the space of a week decided to relinquish responsibility for them. Charlie trekked over to the Isle of Wight to collect them, and armed with bin bags galore, full of all of their worldly possessions, they entered our small bungalow on 12th May 2007. Magically, I had gone from three children to six in the space of three months. Once again I look back and think, what happened!!!

We had run out of money to get legal representation, and I spent much of my free time writing letters to the court, solicitor and the CSA. I felt massively honoured that I could provide a good, secure home for all six of my children, no matter what their heritage, and struggled with the idea that another mother could give her children up so readily.

How-ever the court system is long, arduous and filled with pomp! It filled me with dread every time a court letter landed on our door mat. Every six months the absent mother would visit another solicitor with a tale of woe, about how we had stopped her from seeing the children and how we had virtually kidnapped them from her!

The solicitor would duly send us a protracted letter telling us that she wanted access every other weekend, with overnight staying contact, and we, would fire back a twenty-page document with the reasons why we had stopped contact. It was not unusual for the request to be retracted!

This cat and mouse game became the norm. She avoided paying for the children and I worked more on a weekend than ever to make up for our high outgoings.

In February 2011, having been dragged back and forth in the court system we had conceded to supervised contact on a one to one basis. This happened haphazardly, with visits being cancelled at the last minute. This is what we were so desperate to avoid, given that both children were adverse to uncertainty.

They would wake on alternate Saturdays not knowing if the contact was going to take place or not. We were pushing for psychological testing and hair strand analysis to be done to ascertain if there was a personality disorder and issues with alcohol with the children's mother. The court and CAFCASS (Children and Family Court Advisory and Support Service)were favourable to that course of action, however she was fighting against it tooth and nail. I have no issues with people wanting to drink and having a personality disorder, but where my young charges were concerned, I wanted to know what we were dealing with.

The children's CAMHS (Children and Adolescent Mental Health Service) psychologist had written us a favourable letter detailing that contact was not in the best interest of the children until their mother could address her issues, and we held onto this tightly, like it was our winning lottery ticket. Both children had been under the Mental health team for two years due to issues with behaviour, risk taking and abandonment.

Throughout the next few months there was court appearance after court appearance. I was working every weekend as a midwife, my husband lived away during the week and we had little time together, and the little time that we had on a weekend was spent debating court issues and the progress of the case. Looking after the children was exhausting and I was reaching rock bottom. As the main carer, sorter and the one who felt whole heartedly responsible for all the children, I just wanted the whole debacle to go away! It felt like I had a third person in my marriage that was really not welcome.

The CAFCASS officer visited us one sunny July afternoon to chat to us about her forth coming recommendations in their third report. We were fortunate to have been allocated the one CAFCASS officer with common sense and empathy. Our experience prior to Alison was that the officers had little integrity and were spineless, not wanting to do the right thing, but take the path of least resistance. Alison was the complete anthesis to this. She was loud, effective and actually listened.

She was accompanied by the children's court guardian who was there to make sure that whatever happened was in the children's best interests. She was a great listener who had a kind, gentle demeanour and was called Martha.

The court wanted to make sure that it was not us making the major decisions, but a combined effort of CAFCASS and the Guardian. Our wishes would be taken into account, but were not guaranteed to be enforced. It felt like a precarious time and I felt very out of control.

As we sat outside, kids milling around in front of us, Alison began to tell me that she was contemplating allowing a couple of sessions of supervised contact per year, with weekly phone contact and letter contact too. This was quite the opposite of what we had asked for. We wanted a cessation of all contact until the children turned eighteen and were old enough to deal with their irrational and narcissistic mother themselves.

I felt myself stiffen.

'Do you know what this has been like Alison for the last four years? How difficult it is to be dragged through the courts every six months relentlessly, never able to move on with our lives, everyone disrupted and distraught by the behaviour and demands of her and the court?' I asked as calmly as I could.

The flood gates were open now, I was on a roll as I started to cry.

'Both children have emotional issues and are working with CAMHS, they cannot begin to heal with such uncertainty. My relationship with my husband is suffering beyond belief, all we can focus on a family is court, and frankly its stopping me being a good mum to all six children. If you allow this situation to continue I will leave this family, taking my birth children with me. I cannot do this any-more' I shouted, banging my hands against the wall.

Alison and Martha sat stock still. Alison tried to speak, but Martha stopped her.

'What has this been like for you all?' she gently asked.

That was the first time that anyone had asked just what it was like walking in our shoes for the last torturous four years, and I was shocked and how much it upset me.

'It's hard, it's draining, it's exhausting' I began.

'I want so much to be a mother and a positive figure in the children's lives, but I am so tied up sorting court and worrying about the negative effects of the children spending any time with their mother that I don't sleep.

All we talk about is what nonsense she will spout next, what poisonous crap she will spout to the children if she sees them, and what contact with her will do to them in their later years. I cannot keep doing 'court' anymore. I want to spend time watching all six of my children growing up and making memories, not fighting the court and that crazy woman.

She's proved that she can't parent, that she can't put their needs above that of their own and can-not commit to them one bit, but I can. I love them all so much, but I've had enough. I will walk away if it goes on.' I sobbed.

Martha handed me a tissue, 'I think we understand' she said, knowingly looking at Alison, who looked thoroughly bemused.

'I want to know that we are not going to be dragged back into court time and time, going over the same argument, and I want you to use a 91.14 order' I instructed, soundly like I knew what I was talking about!

'I know that they're rare, but I think that's what we need to stop her taking us back to court all the time. They have been used successfully in the past' I said handing Martha a print out of the order.

'I've heard of it, but never seen it used successfully, but it's worth considering' she contemplated.

For the folks, who haven't spent much time in the family court arena, a 91:14 is a barring order. It can be considered quite a draconian order, but it does have its place. Using this piece of legislation from The Children's Act, it allows a court to stop someone applying back to court for a certain period of time, without them applying for permission from the court to put another application in.

I had come across it late one sleepless night when I was thinking just how much more I could cope with.

'The 91:14 will stop her keep taking us back to court Martha. We could ask that she is barred until the children are 18, or unless she return's back and agrees to the testing and assessments' the legal advisor in me spoke with authority. I had researched well!

'Let me think, we'll be in touch before the next court date' she said, rising up and signalling a stunned Alison that it was time to go.

I felt elated that I had got my point across, but was still anxious and stressed about the impending court session.

We received a court date for September which we duly attended. Charlie took the day off work and the children went to nursery. We were suited and booted, which was laughable given that I wasn't even allowed in the court room, as according to the law, and to the mother's solicitor the case didn't concern me! As their primary carer, I was told by the crazy looking, slightly improper solicitor Jim, that I should go home now, as this didn't concern me.

Thankfully, Martha over heard him, as she waited patiently to get a cup of tea in the busy ante-room outside the crown court, and popped her hand on my shoulder. I so wanted to smack the sanctimonious arsehole over the head with my laden brief case, yet I knew that he was just goading me! Charlie was called into the inner sanctum of the court room and was out again within a few minutes.

'She didn't come, apparently she's in Germany on business. They're going to set a new date and let us know the date. Martha has asked the judge to consider the 91:14 that you mentioned to her. The judge wasn't impressed that she didn't come, you know. He's going to instruct without her if she doesn't get her ass in gear and come to the next hearing!' Charlie relayed.

I was shocked and angry. Once again, she'd caused so much inconvenience and couldn't even be bothered to get to a hearing that concerned the future of the contact with her children. Charlie, ever patient was happy to wait until the next court date. To this day he is amazing at playing the long game.

We set about decorating our new house, and began some major building works to build another bedroom, so that the older girls were not sharing with Loola, who was only five! It wasn't ideal, but we managed. With the new bedroom built and decorated I took a rare, child free day to begin revamping the older girl's bedroom. It was 11th November 2011. I was wearing my manky, dirty decorating clobber and had my hair piled in a messy knot on my head.

I was up the step ladder around 08.40 when the home phone rang. I couldn't be bothered to answer it, I had a room to paint before it was school pick up time. It rang for a good while before it stopped. A few moments later my mobile buzzed from its resting place on the window sill.

Clearly someone wanted to get hold of me! Sighing loudly and chuntering to myself I picked up, not recognising the number.

'Is that Mrs Downey?' the familiar voice asked.

'Yes, Martha, is that you?' I answered, feeling my knees go weak at the adrenaline rush that flooded through my body, at the thought of court and such like.

'Where are you both, we're due in court at 9am'

My heart stopped, 'Sorry? We didn't get a letter. I'm painting and Charlie is in Basingstoke where he works, it will take him three hours to get home!' I told her.

'We so want this over Martha, we would never deliberately not come. We've never missed a hearing before, not even when Lolly was nine days old!' I began to cry.

'Let me deal with it, I'll speak to the court and be in contact shortly' she reassured me with her calm, authoritative tone.

I absolutely knew that they would adjourn the case again and the whole shenanigans would continue for another three months, right over Christmas and New Year. I couldn't think of a worse outcome, I had hoped that in time for the New Year we may have had a resolution and could begin to move on. Sadly now, this seemed unlikely. I called Charlie at work in Basingstoke and cried at the injustice of it all. He was philosophical about the whole thing, as is his way.

'We're nearly there' was all he would say!

How he remained so calm, I will never know! I was so stressed by our whole life, that the court was, I was sure, going to be the straw that broke the camel's back.

Pity party over, I began to paint. Erasing a gross, peach, seventies colour with a warm beige and cream. Up and down the step ladder, in total automaton I went, unaware of the hours that were passing me by. No phone call was forth coming, and I surmised that no news, was good news.

Shortly before 4pm I began to clear up the devastation in the room, ready for school pick up. In 2011, I was quite behind the times, and used email as little as possible, finding it impersonal and time consuming. Unusually for me, I checked my emails as I changed my painty outfit for more befitting mummy pick up clothes and gasped as I clicked open an email from Martha, the solicitor.

As I skim read the text I gasped and shook as I read how the mother had not bothered to attend, sending apologies to the court as she was travelling on business, making clear that she would not be consenting to any such tests, psychological or otherwise, at any point.

In response to evidence from Martha, and CAFCASS, who had recommended no contact until the tests were done, the judge had very willingly issued a 91:14, non-contact order until both children had turned eighteen. In a nut shell, Martha explained this meant that Catherine would have to apply for leave of the court (permission, in layman's terms) before she could apply back to court to recommence contact proceedings.

This wholly unused and fairly draconian order had saved us more court appearances, stress and angst. I sobbed as I called Martha in her office and listened as she regaled me with the judge's disgust that 'The Mother' had failed to turn up once again.

'You'll get a letter in the post, but it's over' she reassured, as I sobbed.

'She isn't going to consent to the testing's, she's made that clear, and in that case, she is completely unable to apply back into court for contact until they are done. It really is finally over. Please go and celebrate and begin to enjoy your life. Alison and I will come out and speak with the children to explain to them about the court's decision, as we feel that it is important that they know that this was not your decision, but ours.'

We hung up, and my gratitude to this calm, amazing solicitor remains, to this day to be immense. She was prepared to buck the system, and take a chance on us, and use a most unused piece of law in order to give us our life back.

Regaining composure, I called Charlie and told him the news. He was stunned into silence. No words were necessary and the easy silence between us said a thousand words of relief and gratitude. Finally, after a very long six years we could move on with our lives, be the parents that we wished to be and enjoy our children before they grew up and flew the nest.

Chapter 29 Moving On

That Christmas and New Year we celebrated and drank to good health, family and a relaxing and less stressful 2012. As we sat, sipping champagne on New Year's Eve, watching the fireworks from our high up vantage point on the side of the Malvern Hills, we toasted each other, our love, our family and our future.

The winter turned to Spring and the children grew and blossomed. I truly believe that happy parents mean happier children. I still parented, Monday to Friday alone, but was in a routine and was enjoying my new career in the Domestic Abuse industry.

The pay was pants, but it gave me back my weekends, was flexible and I worked alongside a team of passionate and feisty men and women, who like me, wanted to wipe out the parasite of Domestic Abuse. I had gained confidence in my abilities, no longer believing that I was a one trick pony midwife, but a capable advocate for the clients I worked with.

I had no problem challenging the police, Children's Services and solicitors with whom I worked on a daily basis, always professional, but ready to counter the ineptitude and rash conclusions that were made about women, to whom such revolting acts of violence and control were perpetrated.

I began to notice that so many of my clients came from a back ground of abuse, broken homes, abandonment and in finding themselves in a thoroughly unsuitable relationship, toxic on every level, often had not the support system to leave, and found themselves stuck in a cycle of power and control. I was grateful that I, as a child had run away from the house in which there were such dreadful memories of such horrible abuse.

I woke up every weekend immensely grateful for our time together, often in awe that I wasn't having to work another weekend. Yet I kidded myself that the lack of money was not a problem, and that as I had used so often 'it would all work it out in the end'. I didn't realise that money is as vital as oxygen, and that without it your children went without and bills didn't get paid.

Having grown up with very little I wanted to be able to make memories with my children and expose them new things and experiences. Sadly this all took money that I didn't have, thus life became more about existing rather than living. As we got more and more broke I tightened our purses even tighter. I was able to feed a family of eight on £50 a week and withdrew all the children from every payable club that they attended. Did I feel guilty and a failure? Of course, but I did what I needed to do in order to survive.

My new job required a lot of driving between counties, and it was on these drives that I began to have flash backs. Initially, it would be like a short, snap shot, photograph like that filled my brain on my bedroom as a child, in the dark, with me lay on my front with my night shirt raised high above my waist. My father was crouched behind me, touching, probing, muttering to himself. The shadow from the landing light cast a shadow on the floor, and I knew that it was bad, wrong.

Even all those years ago, as I write this for the very first time, as a forty-four-year-old woman, I feel the guilt, the fright and the confusion. In a coffee shop corner where I write this, I swallow down bile and fight the urge to sob, calming myself with my melodic tapping on the key board. The lump in my chest, indescribable, after all these years, perhaps is not as healed as I thought.

In that snap-shot came, years' worth of guilt, of hurt, of denial. I tried to deny the existence of this memory, but once it was there it became clearer, more vivid and did not stay still, but, began to play like a movie. It started to affect my subconscious thoughts and much as I tried to block it out by closing my eyes, which was not a good thing as I drove!

When I made love to my gorgeous husband, who I to this day find phenomenally attractive, the guilt and derision that I felt towards me and to the act of love making, would be infected by the deep-seated anxiety and the realisation that I must have had an orgasm at the hands of my father.

Chapter 30 Pandora's Box

For as long as I had been sexually active I had never had a problem reaching orgasm, yet as the flash backs worsened the moment of orgasm took me back to a dark, terrifying place and left me reeling.

As my love for my husband grew, and as the mental movie that played itself at will in my brain morphed into bright technicolor, so that my panic attacks during orgasm would increase. I would be unable to breathe, feel like my chest was collapsing and sob hysterically.

This clearly killed the moment for us both, and Charlie would be left holding his wreck of a wife. I tried the self-talk, the positive affirmations and the like, but to no avail. The flash backs persisted with vengeance and became more physical in nature. As a woman with a healthy sex drive and a phenomenal amount of lust for her gorgeous husband I realised that I needed some intervention and help to take back my mind and my body.

The video was so real, the sounds, the smells and the physicality of the scene. I knew it was true, yet still partly denied to myself that anything happened. I still have enormous gaps in my child hood memories and conclude that my brain has probably locked so much more horror away in order to protect my wellbeing. I had not asked for such things to arise, but was now in a position to try and deal with the issues from my past and the sins of my father.

Bravely, I took the bull by the horns and phoned WRASAC (the Worcestershire Rape and Sexual Abuse Centre) on November 10th 2011. Just making the call was horrific and my voice shook as I said that I needed to come and get some help.

With swift efficiency, I was invited to attend an assessment, pending a place on the waiting list a few weeks later. It was a huge step to make, yet as I put the phone down I felt liberated and free. In moving forward and taking steps to regain the control back which I had lost, seemed to empower me and inspire me more.

I had a great relationship with my bosses Kate and Zoe in the Domestic Abuse Service and took the time to tell them what I was embarking on and why. They were horrified on my behalf, both remarking how unscathed I seemed on the outside, at least. It was hard to confess to them that I felt functioning mad and felt like I was living in a dream!

With their encouragement I went for my initial assessment. I tossed and turned the night before and had wild and crazy dreams. I tried to make every excuse under the sun to not go for the assessment, yet my rational brain knew that I needed to face this demon head on.

I was virtually sick as I got out of my car, and nearly bottled it with every step. Was it easier just to pretend that the abuse had never happened rather than admit it to myself and a counsellor the true extent of my childhood horrors? Charlie, worried about me took a day off work. I barely spoke on the thirty minute drive to the centre. I had been warned not to tell him the venue, due to strict confidentiality rules, to protect clients and staff, and I joked that if I told him, then I may have to kill him!

He wanted to wait around the corner, in case it all went horribly wrong, yet with some gentle persuasion, that I would be OK, and was not going to fall apart or run away he went to the local garden centre for a coffee. I have never been good at showing vulnerability and whilst I felt like I was breaking apart, piece by piece, I just couldn't bear him to see me so broken.

My legs felt heavy and my heart pounded as I crossed the main road. As I rang the doorbell of the unnamed building my knees shook and I struggled to control my breathing. I thought that I was strong and resilient, yet wondered at that precise moment in time if I could really go through with it. Perhaps it would be better to just call the whole thing off, and go back to living in denial.

Before I could run away, a kind looking woman appeared at the door, introduced herself and ushered me upstairs into a room with a sofa, chairs, comfy cushions and, more importantly, tissues. We got through some basic form filling before she asked me about my experiences, reiterating that I did not have to divulge anything that I was not comfortable with.

I heard myself quantifying my experiences on a personal abuse scale and recall feeling a fraud. I had not been raped, tortured or violently treated by my father and the other abusers. The three recollections of my abuse were, in my head probably worth a 1 or 2 on a scale of 1-10 in my head. I know that this shows the fragility of my thinking and my unwillingness to accept that my experiences had been horrific and distressing.

The kind lady, (I cannot remember her name, and probably couldn't have remembered my own name at that point in time) chatted gently about the validity of my experiences and that I absolutely had every right to come as a service user.

What a juxtaposition it was for me to be labelled a service user, when in my day job, where I was very efficient and fought daily battles to keep my clients safe from harm, they were the service users, yet now the boot was on the other foot and I was seeing things from their perspective. I felt ashamed, anxious and concerned that someone was going to judge me in relation to my abuse and my past.

What if's played merrily along in my mind. 'What if'....... They thought that I was mad and my children were taken from me? What if they said that my abuse wasn't severe enough to warrant counselling? What if they told my family and employers that I was stark raving crackers, that I felt a fraud and a phoney and so lost and isolated at times that I may as well be on a desert island? What if? What if?

Well, unsurprisingly, none of the above occurred at the first session and I was thankfully put on the waiting list. I knew that it could be a good while before a counsellor became available, as there was a shortage of resources, thanks to yet more funding cuts, but I felt a little more in control knowing that I was taking steps to make my world a better place.

I continued along with my life, with the flash backs and panic attacks after sex. I wanted the intimacy that sex gave me, the connection and the closeness, yet the physical and psychological effects afterwards left me feeling more broken than ever. I had hoped for my appointment for counselling to come through quickly, but by Christmas nothing had come through.

Life meandered through New Year and into Spring, During the week I was preoccupied with building works, working, the children and money worries. At weekends I spent time being a wife and trying to fool myself and Charlie that I wasn't slowly falling apart.

Chapter 31 Slaying The Dragon

At the end of April, I got a much-awaited call. It came out of the blue. An appointment had come up for the 4th May 2012 and whilst I was petrified of unleashing the memories that I now saw in my head every day, I was by now desperate to make a change and take hold of my issues, once and for all.

So, with trepidation and much Dutch courage I went to my first appointment, driving alone and knowing that opening the Pandora's box was going to be one of the toughest things I had ever done, but also knowing that the boil needed excising, once and for all. The long drive in to the centre was at rush hour, and the stress of negotiating the busy city roads added to my anxiety and angst. Once more I parked up and dragged my begrudging feet over the crossing to the main front door. I was near to tears before I had even pressed the door bell!

My counsellor appeared from behind the door and introduced herself as Eliza. I was guided through the maze of corridors to a cosy, bright room with sofas and cushions. I placed myself in the small tub chair which had high sides. It made me feel protected and seemed easier to shrink down into. Tucking my legs underneath me, with the cushion atop my knees, I was cocooned into the space.

'Do you want to tell me a bit about why you have come to WRASAC' she started.

I cried as I tried to speak, but no words would come. It was like I had lost the power of speech and for one normally so ready to speak I was inept. The vision of my father abusing me, in that shadowy bedroom was at the front of my mind. The sounds, murmurings, movements were all there, yet I couldn't verbalise it. I instantly felt a failure and like I was wasting Eliza's time. Surely the words would come easier than this?

She skillfully moved the conversation onto the here and now, my life as a mother, as a wife, as a worker and friend. I spoke about my relationship with Charlie, how I loved him desperately, how I was needy, yet tried to be strong and valiant and about how weak I felt when I let him know how needy I actually was. I spoke through sobs about the panic attacks during orgasm and how I watched the video over and over in my mind, unable to find the remote to turn it off.

Eliza took the time to gently tell me that our bodies are conditioned to react to stimulation, even as a child and that my thoughts associated with orgasm and the deep-seated damage was not something that I could control back then, my body was just, in effect, doing as it was told, but now, with some therapy and mindset I could take back ownership of my thoughts, reactions and pleasure and begin to change the patterns.

I spoke about how alone I had felt since divulging my secret to my aunt and mother and how my mother's behaviour towards me had gotten worse, yet all I wanted in the world was to be loved and treated equally. So much poured out

146

of my mouth, it was as if the flood gates had finally opened. She took me through the fundamentals of that relationship to explore the toxicity and hurt which had been part of the dynamics between my mother and I for so long.

I cried more than I could have ever imagined as I sat in that chair, wet, soggy tissue firmly clasped in my sweaty palms. I folded it and unfolded it until it was threadbare and broken. This is exactly how I felt.

All of my old wounds and issues were opened up, raw and infected. I felt dirty and not in the least bit jubilant as I left the building after ninety minutes of counselling. The effect on my body was such that I felt complete exhaustion and wanted to go home, crawl away into a hole and sleep for eternity. I do not remember driving home, yet know that the moment I got home I got straight into my warm and cosy bed and did not speak to another soul all evening.

Yet, the mother in me knew that taking to my bed long-term wasn't an option. Zipping up my resilience cloak, I went about my motherly duties in a dazed manner, on automaton, not feeling, just being.

The following day my body reacted to such stress with a migraine and stomach upset. It was like the malevolent poison was seeping through my pores and trying to break me physically too. I called in sick to work, telling Zoe that I never imagined that counselling would be so physically debilitating. She reassured me that I could and would do this. As the week progressed I began to feel less violated, yet as the next session loomed, the same sense of dread reared its ugly head again.

The following week I went back and we covered a little more ground. Despite reassurances from Eliza that I did not have to tell her details of the abuse, I knew that in order to break the spell, I would have to let her into my world. Legs crunched under my body, cushion over my lap and yet another soggy tissue being needed to death in my hands I started to set a scene. I told her that I had always known that things were different, about the black holes in my childhood, about the control and the emotional abuse at the hands of my stepmother, and how I felt so much like the black sheep of the family. No-one else had ever attempted to empathise with my experiences, nor taken time to ask me about them and that played on my mind such a lot.

I have heard of whole families shunning the exposer of abuse, rather than face facts and believe them, and I felt so much that this was happening to me. My mother took the time to write to my father at his house and detail her hatred and distaste for him, yet this focused on her blame of him, rather than her part in leaving me with him in the first place, and never having me back to live with her.

Every subsequent session involved me sobbing and burying my head in a pillow, unable to have Eliza look at me. Yet in an instant I was able to switch into coping mode, and never really let my full guard down. Old habits die hard, and I know it was this ability to never fully reveal my full feelings, good or bad which had kept me safe as a child, yet had kept me trapped in my adulthood in toxic relationships. My ability to be having an internal meltdown which was not obvious to anyone else, I feel is down to my resilience and desire to never quit.

Before my third session I made knew that I had to move things along. I had never envisaged being beholden to therapy for a long period of time and knew that in order to heal and change my world that I needed to share with Eliza exactly what had happened in the bedroom that night, so many years ago. I know of people who have spent many years in therapy, becoming dependant upon it and treating their counsellor like an old friend. This was never part of my plan. I knew that for me therapy was a short lived entity which would allow me to move on fully and be released from the demons in my head.

As I walked up the stairs that afternoon I told Eliza that I had had a chat with myself and that I was going to just get on with telling my story. I knew what I needed to do, and with cushion covering my face, I began to tell her from start to finish how I had been woken up, sexually abused both rectally and vaginally and how it had gone on and on. In that moment I remembered more detail than I ever thought possible. I recalled my thoughts, disgust and embarrassment. At my bewilderment, yet acceptance at yet another man who hurt and assaulted me.

I wept tears of what had been, and tears for what should have been. The tale went on and on, and what I had thought was only a two second clip, morphed into a twenty minute tale of perversion. I shouted and screamed into my pillow at the injustice of my childhood, how being left alone with some pervert had nearly destroyed me and how sad and angry I was with both of my parents. Eliza, coaxed more and more out, giving me permission for the first time in many years to vent fully.

I knew that I should only be angry at my father, being the perpetrator, yet for the first time ever I became angry at my mother for leaving me with him and for never, despite my tears and angst living in the house offered me the chance to go and live in her unbelievably happy home. Eliza allowed me the space and time to work through my feelings, without judgement or question. She was never shocked or judgmental. My words, for the first time flowed, relentless and at the end of my allotted hour, Eliza asked if I wanted to continue. With child care sorted, I was under no time constraints, which was a rarity and I was desperate to unleash the beast just a little more.

We began to work through the relationship with my father in depth, exploring his control and misogyny. Working backwards, I could pin point how he tried to keep my inner spirt quashed with ridicule, anger and control, He was desperate to not let me grow up and hated me questioning him over anything. He was the ultimate womaniser and had innumerable affairs, with women who thought he was a catch. He could be convincing, kind, caring and loving, until, they tried to push against his controlling ways. It was bizarre though, I thought, how desperate I was for him to find another woman to live with, given the hatred that my stepmother belayed upon me.

I recalled to Eliza, how I had actively encouraged him to embark upon an affair with a bridesmaid at a wedding, as she was so kind to me. He would use me as a means to be getting to them and I was often taken to their houses late at night, on errands with him.

I was angry at him for making me have a part to play in his affairs and hated him for making my stepmother hate me even more! I opened up for the first time to anyone, at how, at fourteen I found his porn videos, as I was looking for the biscuit hiding places in his house. I had long moved out, but was forced to go to his house a few nights a week for tea, and was often left alone. On top of the cupboard was a video stash.

Being a nosy kind of teenager, I popped it into the player, knowing that it was probably something that my prying eyes were not meant to see, yet my reckless nature urged me to press play. The video started up and a young-looking girl, dressed in a school uniform was forced into a warehouse.

Glued to the screen I watched as she was roughly forced into sex with two men who roughly raped her anally and vaginally. I felt sick and disgusted.

My father was turned on by porn involving either young school girls, or of women who looked very young and dressed up as school girls. I didn't need to know the truth about the video, I just knew that it was morally reprehensible, disgusting, and that it stirred up old memories in me which I had locked away.

Admitting to a counsellor that my father was a paedophile was harrowing. For over thirty-five years I had kept such secrets locked away, safe from harm and now, faced with the rational voice of Eliza, I knew that was exactly what he was.

My anger boiled over as I spoke of retribution, revenge, the police and the courts. I was petrified back then of taking that step. Fear of prosecution stopped me from driving around to his house, which was minutes from the offices and caving his fucking skull in with a hammer.

As that session came to an end I felt jubilant that I had found the courage to speak out, yet knew that my journey was not over just yet. The exhaustion was both physical and emotional, and as I fell doggedly down the stairs, out of the building and dragged myself to the car I could barely think. The grief and horror of the last two hours had left me numb and ragged. I just wanted to sleep away the pain and let my wounds heal.

As I drove home I played the snap shot video over in my mind, and for the first time in many years, I noticed that it had lost its intensity. It seemed less vivid, and the colours slightly muted, as if someone had messed with the brightness and volume button.

In the days that followed, my home became my castle and I struggled to leave it, unless I had to. I just wanted familiarity, calm and the bodies of my husband and children around me 24/7.

Not many of my friends knew about my weekly counselling appointment, yet the two who I confided in were empathetic and asked for no details from me. My mother and aunt knew that the counselling was ongoing, yet offered no counsel or interest into my progress.

Eliza's perspective on this, was that it was my mother's guilt which stopped her from showing compassion and love. This seemed contrary to me, given that my mother had concluded that 'she had nothing to apologise for to me and no guilt to carry'.

Once again, to hear that opinion from an outsider, one not associated with my family, was revolutionary and began to open my eyes into the peculiar world of our 'mother, daughter relationship'. The truth of my world was beginning to reveal itself and would have far reaching consequences for both me and my children.

Chapter 32 The Letter

The weeks flew by with the usual litany of juggling many balls with my busy, chaotic family and job. Before I knew it, it was Wednesday again and time for me to go and open my soul. With the details of the abuse out in the open we spent the next few weeks breaking open my confusion and heart ache that I felt towards my mother.

We took the relationship right back to the 70's when she and my father married. They were eighteen and nineteen, both immature and not able to look after a dog, let alone a five-week premature baby. I spouted the stories that I had been told, about my mother leaving and my father's vicious battle to retain custody of me.

My mother, according to the court papers had left my father for another man and made little attempt to keep me. She was young, I had always rationalised, and though she had always maintained that she had thought that she was doing the best thing by me, as a mother I struggled to accept this anymore.

As a devoted and dedicated mother, who had readily taken on another woman's two small children, and would die without a moment's hesitation for any one of them, I questioned just why she left me, tiny and vulnerable with a man she knew to be controlling and abusive and never came back for me at any point. It seems harsh to be judging her actions which had been made so may years ago, but part of my healing was to dismantle my past and put together the pieces.

We spoke about being a child and feeling left out and different compared to my siblings in Wales, and how this disparity had been brushed aside when I tried to bring up the inconsistencies which were still rife in our relationship to that day.

I had been labelled prickly, difficult and hard to be around by both my mother and sister, yet had never had any difficulties in making or maintaining relationships. I shared my thoughts with Eliza, who would reflect them back to me and ask if I thought that what had been said or implied to me, was really a reflection of me or those who acted so unkindly and without empathy.

It was a hard thing to explain to a stranger just how I had wanted to be accepted and loved by my mother, and how I worked my ass off to make her love me, doing practical tasks to make her believe that she couldn't live without me. How as a child I cleaned her house daily to get recognition from her and how as an adult I achieved so much, yet rarely got a well done.

I cried as I relived the waiting for phone calls and letters that were promised, yet never delivered and at how I readily accepted the excuses. How I tried to stop calling her to see how long it would be before she remembered to call me, and after nearly four weeks I capitulated and phoned her to see if I had been missed.

It was a bizarre game of cat and mouse and one which I was aware was psychologically destructive. For the first time ever, sharing my deepest and often darkest thoughts was cathartic and petrifying.

Telling Eliza how my mother chose to never pay a penny towards me, ever, not even when I ran away from home at thirteen to live with her sister, yet openly chastised her ex-husband who was a reluctant payer of maintenance, yet she never saw the irony of her own situation.

I was always too afraid to rock the boat with our relationship for fear that if I pushed her into a corner and called out her behaviour's how I might kill the relationship once and for-all and give her just the excuse she needed to walk away.

Chapter 33 One Toe Over The Line

I was strong in that room, yet the moment I got into the car I lost my courage. It was better in my eyes to have a tiny piece of her in a relationship, than be totally isolated. I was happy to remain being the hard working, compliant girl that I had always been, trying to achieve so much to get respect from her and yet, always striving to make her proud. It seemed that the more I achieved, to me, the less impressed she was.

I had trained as a midwife, got a diploma, a degree, renovated three houses, was bringing up six children, survived a divorce, was resourceful and strong, yet she seemed to want me to be weak and needy, the two things that I swore that I never would be.

I asked for little from her. It seemed to me that had I been a psychological liability, as statistics seemed to point towards, with a history of sexual abuse, neglect and a background of a broken home I should by all accounts be dysfunctional at best, or an addict of some description with my children in care that she would have rallied around after me! Yet somehow I had defied the statistics.

I was not dependent upon drugs, alcohol, cigarettes, a violent relationship and was not on prescription anti-depression meds.

I had never had a victim mindset, instead making a choice to adopt a positive and passionate view of life, choosing to turn negatives into positives and succeed in everything that I did. It comes back to resilience once again. The desire to keep getting back up and never allowing ANYTHING to get in the way of my chosen path. The ability to see the good in situations and see the beauty in my life.

Eliza listened, reflected but never offered her opinion. I trod a path well-travelled in that small, cosy room that was riddled with sadness and came to my own conclusion that I deserved more from my mother. That I had no choice as I approached my fortieth birthday but to change to balance of our relationship, ask her for more and accept that in doing so I ran the absolute risk of her closing the door on the relationship for good. I knew that my mother did not suffer criticism well and would come back venomously.

As I have already disclosed to you, I had never set out to have counselling for a long period of time. For me it was a tick in the box to help me with my recovery, and I know in reflection I needed a professional to acknowledge my abuse in order to admit to myself that I had been abused. So, feeling strong and jubilant in August of that year, after ten sessions I left therapy and began to seek ways to change my relationships for the better.

I started by writing to my mum, laying my thoughts on paper. I had never verbalised my anxieties, my sadness and my desire to be considered a real daughter before, and as I committed my thoughts down that this was a cross roads in our relationship.

My six-page, hand written letter was open, honest and full of hope. I owned my observations and tried to back my thoughts up with examples. It was assertive and ended with the line

'I drew the short straw when it came to fathers and don't want to have to come to the same conclusion that you are a poor mother. I deserve more.'

It didn't pull any punches, yet I hoped that she would read it and that it would be the start of a loving and happy relationship where I felt worthy, wanted and where she realised just how much I loved her and needed her in my life.

I posted the letter as I departed for a week's camping with six children in West Wales. As I write this there are so many things that are fundamentally wrong with this sentence. Camping, with six children, in West wales!! Was I crazy? Yep, it seems so. But we were broke and this was going to be a holiday filled with memories!. We set off knowing that the area is more prone to monsoon weather than sun and heat, yet the mood was buoyant in our old charabanc car which was rammed to the hilt.

I experienced some flashes of terror and anxiety as we got further from home. The counselling had rendered me useless for many months, becoming virtually agoraphobic and desperately needy unless I was around my solid, calm husband and for the first time in a while we were venturing away from my sanctuary where I felt safe and warm. I thought about the response my mum may have to the letter and what her next course of action might be, yet as our wet, cold week progressed there was no call and no contact.

The site was heavily waterlogged and our pitch a quagmire of sticky mud and a haven for mosquitos. With only a 2 burner camping stove, I took to lighting the open fire pit every night and cooking on the fire as my young family sat hungrily around in their chairs awaiting their next meal. It bore a resemblance to my vision of life in prehistoric times, with hunter gatherers cooking their mammoth meat on open fires and men spending days hunting for the next meal with a sharpened spear.

If you've not cooked on an open fire and watched the flames dance and spit in front of you, smelt the newly cut logs as they burnt and realised that you too smell of charcoal, soot and smoke then I recommend that you book a simple holiday to make you realise just how comfy your bed is, how warm your shower is and how convenient your kitchen is. It is liberating, yet exhausting!

As the kids roamed feral in the acres of safe woodland, chopped logs with axes the same size as them and learnt to whittle wood into all manner of things I began to panic about my actions. I think even back then, I knew that the die was cast and that my mother would take my actions as a sign of disrespect rather than a cry to make our relationship more balanced and healthy.

By the end of the sixth day, with leaky tents, muddy clothes and damp beds we threw in our wet towels and decided to make the long 2 car journey home. Being poor meant that we couldn't afford an eight-seater car, so two cars were necessary to transport 2 tents, 6 kids, eight beds, eight chairs, bedding, food, clothes and other chattels home. I recall that I did twenty-two loads of washing to clean the smoky, muddy mess from all things fabric. It was a grateful distraction from the waiting game that ensued as I held on for a response from my mother.

Eventually two weeks later a hand written letter arrived on my mat. It was conciliatory in places, yet mainly apportioned blame to me. I was difficult, needy and wanted such a lot. It didn't particularly deal with the points that I raised in my letter, but ended with a ' I love you very much, you were my first born.'

In all honesty I was not sure that very much was achieved from my letter, save that my mother now had in her eyes more grounds to not see much of me.

Chapter 34 A Worrying Saturday

In June 2013 my nan called me early one Saturday morning. I was busy with the kids and was probably a little rushed. It's no excuse, and I hate myself for being a little curt as I answered the phone.

My nan called me generally once a day to check we were OK, check the weather and to check that I'd wrapped the children in appropriate clothing! If she couldn't raise me on the home phone she'd hunt me down on my mobile, phoning every five minutes in a kind of stalker-ish way, until I put down what-ever I was doing and answered my phone!

That morning was different. I sensed a panic in her voice as she, nan, told me that she had called for the doctor as she had chest pain again. I did indeed put down what I was doing and I was at her house in just over fifteen minutes. Thankfully the roads were kind and not filled with drivers out to look at our beautiful scenery.

My paternal grand-mother, like my maternal nan was a beautiful, warm hearted soul. It was apparent to all who knew and loved her that she appeared to have a serious issue with hypochondria. We joked about having her own seat in the doctors waiting room and woe betide anyone who dared to open her doctors stash cupboard, full of pills and potions that the GP had given her over the years for every illness she had manifested. She went to the GP once a week and I think loved the attention. She knew all the receptionists by name and was loved by her kind GP.

In a loveless life with my cantankerous grandfather she lucked in that Saturday morning as it was her kind and caring female GP who she had called upon that morning. I took one look at her as I walked into the familiar living room and knew that something was not quite right. She looked sallow and was very breathless.

'Can you pack me a bag, Dand, before the ambulance comes' she asked, not wanting to leave my clueless grandfather rooting around in her pants drawers!

I ran upstairs and threw together a bag of night clothes, comfy trousers and a top, toiletries and her photo of her beloved grand children from by the bed.

I was still none the wiser to her condition when the two manned ambulance arrived to take her to hospital.

'Your chariot awaits nan,' I said buoyantly. 'Let's get you checked out.'

With that, she was wheeled out of the house, leaving my grandfather to lock up, and me arranging to meet them both at our local hospital a few minutes away.

In true NHS efficiency we were whisked to a ward straight away and so began a day full of tests. My nan, petrified of hospitals held my hand and asked me to explain to the many doctors just what she felt like and what medication she was on. My grandfather, ever the impatient sat by the bed, seemingly begrudging nan the attention, asking when she could come home.

By the evening it became apparent that she had suffered a minor heart attack and had some respiratory issues. She was still however, her jaunty, inappropriate self, laughing and joking with me and telling me that she couldn't wait to get home into her own bed. As she fell asleep, I stroked her hand and hair and reflected at the role change, that inevitably occurs when child turns to adult, and carer morphs into dependant.

We sent my grandfather home to eat and I sat and read by the bedside until I was ushered away by the nurses around 10 pm. I was reluctant to leave her, but honestly had no idea how sick she was to become.

The following day I arrived on the ward to find my father around the bed. Not wanting to cause a scene or be tempted to punch him, I loitered in the hospital foyer with other people, milling about, buying over priced food in the awful canteen and watching my clock until my father had sloped off again. My sister stayed and we, while not speaking much, had an easy silence.

The doctors and nurses deferred to me, given my medical back-ground and nan proudly told them that I was a midwife. This did seem to give me some credibility with them and they seemed much more open to me helping care and monitor my beautiful nan.

Later that afternoon, nan began to complain of difficult breathing. She got a little paler and although my sister and I propped her up on pillows she became agitated and uncomfortable. She was greyish to look at and her nails were purple. Without asking I grabbed the finger oxygen monitor and popped it onto nans skinny finger and popped the oxygen mask, which was plugged in behind the bed near her face. I went to find a nurse and asked for a doctor to be called immediately. Two nurses were making beds in a bay next to my nans room and promised that they would come as soon as they had finished the bed and that a doctor would be called imminently.

Nan's oxygen levels had risen a little with the oxygen mask on, but she remained clammy, anxious and irritated. As I watched the clock and heard the nurses laughing in the corridor I knew that we were not a priority and that a doctor wasn't appearing anytime soon.

Without fear of wanting to be labelled as an awkward relative I strode back into the hall to the nurses office and asked if the doctor had been called. It was now thirty minutes after nan had taken a turn for the worst and I was not standing by and watching a bunch of apathetic and inefficient staff do nothing as her condition deteriorated.

'My grand-mother needs a doctor NOW', I assertively asked, fluently slipping into medical jargon.

'Her oxygen levels are low, she's cyanosed, her peripheral circulation is poor and she's very agitated and complaining that she can't breathe. I've put your oxygen on and sat her up, BUT, she needs a doctor NOW.'

I waited while the nurse bleeped the doctor and followed the sheepish nurse back to nan's bedside.

'Are you OK Mrs S?' the nurse asked nan, obviously shocked at how sick she had become so quickly.

My normally impeccably mannered nan barely acknowledged the nurse and continued to thrash around in the bed, trying to breathe. It was harrowing to watch. The nurse and I helped nan to sit up more and she recorded some observations onto her charts. I tried to remain calm, but looking at the fast deterioration I was very worried.

After what seemed like a long while a junior doctor was called. He looked like he was barely old enough to shave, yet alone assess patients, however his bedside manner was confident and professional.

He set out examining nan thoroughly, looking at her nails and oxygen readings and his expression became one of concern which I picked up on.

'I'd like to take a small sample of blood,' he said calmly.

I knew that he meant to do an 'arterial stab' to measure more accurately her oxygen levels and how much acid was in her system. It was a difficult and painful procedure. The doctor prepared nan and asked for her consent to take a little sample of blood!! I wasn't in a position to argue about informed consent with him, but braced myself and nans hand for the inevitable needle to assault her tender skin, in the gap between the hand and wrist where the artery runs deep under the skin.

Being as gentle as he could he began to stab the needle deep into the skin. Nan instinctively flinched and moved her hand as the doctor tried hard to draw blood, moving the needle slightly at a different angle each time. Each time the reluctant syringe failed to fill and nan's distress became obvious. In full protective mode I whispered to him,

'You've got one more try then you go and get an anaesthetist' I commanded, taking no prisoners and being unconcerned about his feelings.

'I can do it, 'he said, sweat forming on his forehead as I held down nan's hand and tears rolled down my cheeks. Watching someone that I loved so dearly being hurt was horrific, but eventually he drew the blood and it was whisked off to the lab. Nan was given some drugs to calm her down and oxygen to help her to breathe and seemed to settle a little.

A short time later I was called into the nurse's office by the doctor. With a grave expression he told me that my nans blood picture showed that she had suffered another heart attack and that her blood was very acidic.

This explained her grey pallor, cyanosed fingernails and panicky demeanour. The doctor explained that it was quite likely that she may have another heart attack and that this one had done irreversible damage to her body. They were planning on moving her upstairs to a ward and that the next few days would prove critical.

Shell-shocked, partly because I had not seen this coming at all and through tiredness and exhaustion I stayed with nan until around 1am, then once she was settled bade her good-night. She was sleepy as I kissed her soft cheek and hugged her gently. Despite the odour of the hospital, she still smelled like nan.

I went home to my familiar, warm bed, but before getting in went around and checked on my six babies, all warm and snug in their beds, gently snoring, surrounded by teddies. As I slipped in next to Charlie, listening to the peace and quiet of the house I prayed again to whatever divine power was out there to keep nan safe and help her make a speedy recovery. I was not sure that my heart would survive losing another grandma.

The night flew by and I was awake early to get the children delivered safely to school. By 8am they were safely ensconced in their classrooms, or were on the school bus, mostly oblivious to my heavy heart and difficult decisions that I was going to have to face as I drove to my nans house. I hadn't called the hospital for an update, knowing that it was shift handover and that no one would be free to talk to me, but knew that Grandad would have called at around 5am when he got up.

Grandad was up and about, with no idea about the second heart attack or the gravity of nan's condition. He had called the ward early to find that she was going to move wards, that she would be reviewed by the consultant a little later and she had slept. It was typical nurse jargon for 'get off the phone, I'm quite busy!'

Chapter 35 Opening Up Old Wounds

As nan was not getting better, I spoke to Grandad about the whereabouts of my aunt Anne who I had not had any contact with for around thirty years.

For reasons best known to her, she had moved out of home at seventeen to pursue a career in the NHS and made infrequent visits to see my grand-parents, despite my nan crying and begging her to visit on a more regular basis, as opposed to once every five years. Strangely, she had refused to give them a contact number, nor an address so finding her, to make her aware of nan's deterioration would prove hard.

I asked Grandad for any clues about where she lived and he recalled the town where she was now a district nurse. He gave me his blessing to try and get a message to her to see if she could come down immediately. I knew that my nan would want her present and that she had a right to know.

Feeling like I was opening a Pandora's box, yet fully accepting that I had no other choice I dialled 101 and asked the police to transfer me to the control room to see if they may be able to track down. I explained to the control room operator that I believed that my nan was very poorly, with a poor prognosis, and strange as it was, we, the family had no contact details for her. I left my number with them, and having done as much as I could, hung up. I knew that my involving the police in tracking down my aunt would not be looked upon favourably.

I could never have predicted just how one decision, made with the best of intentions could ever have caused such a manifestation of hate towards me.

At the hospital later, that morning I helped the nurses wash and tend to nan, whilst Grandad entertained anyone who would listen with a list of his ailments and a tale of his hard life. He missed being the centre of attention and I knew that he couldn't interpret the medical jargon used by the doctor, on their ward round so spent a lot of time filling in the gaps for him.

It was during the visiting hours that I came face to face with my sister, brothers, stepmother and my dad for the first time in a very long time. I was not going to let old wounds fester and upset nan, so informed my sister what had happened, the doctor's plan's and that I had asked the police to locate Anne.

Not wanting to speak with my father any more than was necessary, I asked her to relay this to my father. I knew that she has no idea of the reason for my absolute distaste of the man. I popped in and out of the ward, making excuses for phone calls and cups of tea, and whilst off the ward around 2pm had an incoming call from a number I didn't recognise. Heart in my mouth, hands shaking, I accepted the call, knowing who it was before the caller spoke.

'Dani, the police found me in work, you didn't need to do that, they told me about nan' came the opening tirade from Anne. Her voice sounded harsher than I remember and there was little sign of warmth or worry.

'What's been going on with her', she asked nonchalantly.

I told her about the heart attack, chest pain, inability to breathe and anxiety and how she was worsening every day. In my usual door mat manner I apologised for asking the police to find her, explaining meekly that I felt we had no other choice.

'They came to my work, she's a bloody hypochondriac anyway' she moaned, labouring the point. Turning tac, she began to plan to make the eight-hour journey that afternoon. Curtly, she informed me that she would be down later that evening and that she would sort out somewhere to stay once she was down. I hoped that she wouldn't upset nan, or cause an argument with Grandad, as was often par for the course with their relationships.

Grandad was relieved when I told him that the police had located Ann and that she would be down that evening. He seemed to have a much better relationship with him, than nan, for reasons only known to her.

Late that evening she arrived at the hospital. She had morphed into a woman in her fifties, with a prickly, hard demeanour. She greeted Grandad with a hug and paid little attention to nan, lay asleep in her bed.

'Where are the doctors'? she asked.

'I'll fill you in while the staff hand over ready for the night shift' I replied amicably, switching into medical jargon to explain nan's sudden deterioration and the medics concerns.

'She's just got anxiety, for god's sake, always was a bloody hypochondriac', she muttered under her breath, loud enough for me to hear. It was the second time in a short time that I had heard her say such a thing.

'She couldn't breathe, her oxygen saturations (sats) were 82%, this wasn't anxiety' I retorted, refusing to be bullied by this brusque, uncaring being.

'You can go now, I'll stay the night with her,' she offered.

'I'm not ready to go yet thanks. Ill stay a while and check she's settled' was my response.

I stayed for another few hours, until the early hours and as nan's observations were stable made my way to my silent house, littered with toys with my six charges breathing quietly in their warm snug beds, and my husband's warm body snuggled on my side of the bed. Before I knew it, the morning was upon me, and the small forms of my youngest children slid into bed for a cuddle.

Their small, cold hands and feet and warm, soft bodies were comforting as I smelled their freshly washed hair and kissed their soft skin. They pressed for breakfast and CBeebies and leaving daddy snoozing I gave in and got up.

We breakfasted and played, waiting for the other four to rise and as the noise level reached a crescendo I showered and dressed. My thirty second shower woke me up, as I turned it to cold and dressed for another day at the hospital.

Chapter 36 The Sin's

Leaving Charlie to sort the school run and nursery drop I kissed all of them goodbye and left for the hospital, preparing myself for an argument with the staff about it not being visiting on the ward. Wild horses could not and would not drag me away.

The ward was quiet as I stealthily crept into the bay where nan was still sleeping The staff were doing hand over in an office, so no-one saw me sneak in behind the curtain. I kissed her warm face and hand, loving her familiar smell and told her I loved her. She opened her eyes, recognition kicking in and squeezed my hand. I offered her water, and she greedily sucked hard on the straw to quench what was an obvious thirst, after I helped her to scooch up the bed, onto the pillows.

Anne and a nurse I had not seen before entered the bed space behind the curtain and seemed shocked to see me. Strangely though, the nurse did not query my presence, but asked Anne and I if we wanted to go and get a coffee while she gave nan a bed bath. I was sure that nan would rather the nurses bathed her than us, so we readily agreed. Anne decided to drive down the road to Grandad's to shower and freshen up and I promised her that I would call her if anything else happened.

'Do you want to stay at mine tonight, you could meet Charlie and the kids, we've got room' I offered.

'No, it's ok, you've got enough to do, I'll book into a hotel' she declined.

'It's no problem, and the kids would love to meet their great aunt, all the way from Scotland'.

'Are you sure?' she seemed genuinely surprised by my offer.

'Absolutely, you go get showered and collect Grandad and I'll see you in a bit' I said, hugging her.

She gave an impassioned hug back and left the building. A warm spark lit in my heart. A member of my family with whom to build a relationship with was an exciting prospect. I had no idea at that point just how toxic this relationship was to become, within only a few short weeks.

Nan was comfortable and slept as the doctors did their ward round. They were hopeful that she was on the mend, and within a few days might be going home. I was so pleased to hear this and began to plan taking the children to see her once she was back in her house. My sister arrived, and we popped off the ward for a coffee. It was lovely to see her and chat. We had been fairly close when she was younger and I vocalised to her how happy I was to be spending time with her after many years, albeit in less than ideal circumstances.

Looking back, I realise now that I was wearing my heart on my sleeve a little too much. The thought of being part of a cohesive family and feeling like I belonged again left me indescribably happy. Despite nan being ill, I was looking for the positives in what was a desperately dark situation.

I planned to pop home later that afternoon, to collect the children from schools and cook supper. My father, brothers and stepmother had come back to visit, and I knew that we were taking the piss with visiting numbers, so made the excuse to leave, saying that I would come back around 8pm.

The afternoon and evening continued with its usual parental monotony, of homework, supper, nagging for showers and dog walking. Much as I loved them desperately it was bloody hard, thankless work. Cooking for eight was like feeding an army of hungry gannets.

No sooner had they eaten they demanded pudding! It was incessant. Lunch boxes made and a load of washing put-on I got dressed ready to leave the house in order to make my way back to the ward. Grabbing a quick kiss from Charlie as I left the house as he entered back from work I left for the hospital again, not realising that this evening was to hold one of the biggest revelations for me, ever.

Back on the ward, I found my father and Anne, not speaking with a caustic atmosphere of tension tangible between them. She rippled hatred and venom toward him, but I had no idea of the reasons why. Nan seemed unsettled, her breathing laboured again, and she fidgeted in the bed, occasionally clutching her chest, and gasping. It was in contrary with her peaceful form earlier that day.

'Let's get the doctor back, she looks dreadful' I said, as I moved towards the corridor to find a member of staff. Nurse found and my request for a doctor, poste-haste initiated I headed back to the bedside. I couldn't bear to be anywhere near my father and frankly wanted to batter him, however here was neither the time, nor the place. He wanted in on the action with nan, yet was only ever rude, defamatory and aggressive to her when she was well.

He frequently called her names and was rude and dismissive toward her. She lent him money, tried to help him all she could, yet he was thoroughly revolting to her. I pulled him up about it, if I happened to be in the house at the same time, and the urge to punch his horrible face in at that time was tremendous, however no-where near the urge I struggled to relinquish my hold around that bed.

Before I gave in to the desire to beat my father to death right there on the ward the Doctor appeared. His initial convivial approach changed as he examined nan, looking at her fingers and listening to her chest. He reached for the oxygen behind her head and popped the mask over her face, as the nurse popped the electronic beepy machine cuff onto her arm and it began to beep and inflate.

'I'm worried about her lungs, she's got an infection and her oxygen levels are very low. I'll start her on intra-venous antibiotics and give her something to make her more comfortable and we'll see how she goes' he told us.

'She will be ok, won't she?' I felt myself once again crying as I spoke, panic taking over as I faced the doctor.

'I really can't say at this point, she's very sick and weak and her body is struggling, but, we're doing all we can' he tried to reassure the crumbling idiot in front of him.

Over the next hour nan was given the antibiotics and drugs to keep her comfortable and oxygen given through nasal prongs up her nose, which she tried repeatedly to remove. I sat and stroked her hand and chatted quietly to her, as my father and Anne stared each other out awkwardly. My father tried to make small talk, prattling on about nan being a hypochondriac, while I tried to pretend that he didn't exist.

As nan settled down a bit, I fought down the anger and calmly asked my father if he should go home for a break. In reality I knew that he was craving a drink, and that by 10pm on a normal day he could be found inebriated after a skin full of whiskey. He was starting to get the shakes and bit my hand off when I suggested he pop home.

With his revolting form gone the toxic atmosphere depleted immediately. Nan seemed more settled and Anne and I took time to pop to the deserted coffee shop in the hospital foyer. We queued at the Costa and waited for the attendant to come back to the counter. As I pondered my empty belly and how many cakes I could feasibly eat Anne stood at my side.

Moving closer, she leaned in, 'Did nan know?' she asked.

I felt myself take a sharp intake of breath, 'What?' I replied, turning slowly towards her and lowering my voice.

'Did nan know about what he did?' she asked hesitantly.

'To who?' I played dead. Not wanting the conversation to continue.

'I know what he did to you. I've known for many years. I noticed the way he looked at you when you were about eight she said without emotion.

My heart stopped and my thoughts froze. It was as if time stood still as the slow realisation dawned on me. I was not mad, I did not make up the abuse, dream it or any such thing. Here was Anne corroborating my story and telling me that she knew what had gone on for years.

I know to you the reader it must seem strange. To be rejoicing and jubilant about your horrific abuse. But, I really did want to turn naked cartwheels.

Obviously turning naked cartwheels in the hospital foyer would have got me arrested or sectioned, but I use this euphemism to describe the joy that I felt at this moment. I was not alone and for one felt that I had something in common with a member of my family.

I can understand now the power of other victims of abuse realising that they were not alone when the tales of Jimmy Saville abuse came to light. They must have, like me felt totally isolated, and I guess there in lies the power of the abuser. In keeping victims isolated the perpetrator keeps control, reduces the chances of disclosure and of them being believed. This was me! Alone, now not alone! Afraid, now not afraid. Mad, but not really mad!!

As I came to my senses I turned to Anne, who was looking dumb struck at her own revelations. She looked pale and far less calm than me.

'How did you know?' I tentatively asked.

'I've known for many years. I saw him touch you in a way that I knew wasn't right, but who did I tell?

'As she told me her story, I felt sick. I felt mad. I wanted to hurt him all over again for his despicable behaviour. My heart ached for my younger self, but my soul searched for revenge at that point.

I found myself thanking Anne for sharing her story with me and whilst I experienced white rage, it simmered gently below the surface whist the bizarre feeling of joy, which emerged from the revelations that I was not mad or crazy, made me feel lighter and calmer.

As I walked back to my car with the early morning sun bright in the blue sky, I called my mum. I was desperate for her to know about the latest revelations. I can't put my finger on why. Maybe I felt that she may love me more if there was someone else to verify my abuse? Maybe she would believe me more and warm to me just a bit? The answer to that conundrum eludes me to this day, and even as I write I can't fathom why I so needed to share this with my aunt or mum, or why it mattered so much.

I didn't wait for idle chit chat, but launched straight in with, 'You will never guess what Anne told me last night?'

I regaled her with our heart to heart over the Costa counter and explained to her just how this news had made me feel.

'I am not alone, and I am not the only one. I am not mad or bad!' I mused. I asked her to fill my aunt in with the details and she promised to do so.

That night I invited Anne to come and stay with us. She was talking about finding a hotel room to stay in, as she was not keen on staying with my grandfather, yet I would hear nothing of the sort. With nan only seeming a little better and more stable I was excited to introduce my family to my new found aunt.

As we made our way back to the beautiful hills where my house lay I mulled over how excited the children would be to meet the aunt they knew little about and who spoke in a foreign accent. Once inside I began to introduce all six children to Anne and they fussed and rallied around her, sharing my excitement. She was not good with displays of physical affection and was not in the least demonstrative, yet I didn't mind. As the children, hearts open and ready to give love to a perfect stranger kissed her goodnight, my heart glowed with pride at my beautiful family and at their strength of character.

The following morning we both went back to the hospital. It was a beautiful day, yet nan looked worse. She was agitated and pale, with oxygen on her face in a mask and drips in her arm. The nurse reported that her oxygen levels were dropping and they couldn't work out why. Her breathing was becoming more laboured and the nurse was waiting for the ward round with the consultant, whose arrival was imminent. Ann did the bare essentials for nan, with little affection or grace. She chatted to the nurse, who by now realised that I was a midwife and that Anne was a nurse.

Our jobs were the first thing that the nurse reported to the Consultant and his entourage. In my opinion there is no issue with show boating with a consultant. Having a status in the medical world and being able to speak the lingo meant that we got answers quicker, stopped the bull shit and ensured that nan got great care. It was almost as if there was a deeper level of respect from them to us. I was happy to use whatever creative means to get nan exemplary care.

The consultant told us that they were worried as nan's breathing was worsening and she couldn't maintain her oxygen saturations adequately. He explained that he thought her lungs were giving up. It was a bizarre, surreal conversation, given that nan was breathing and conscious in the bed below him!

His answer to the problem was fit nan with an uncomfortable, bulky mask which fixed tightly over the mouth and nose and positively forced oxygen in to the lungs. This contraption, he explained would give her tired lungs a rest and would hopefully help her to get well again.

BUT, he was careful to say, that if this mask didn't improve things, then the prognosis was very poor indeed! This were words that I could not and would not accept and I cried noisily as he explained his treatment. The thought that nan may die was not one that I could comprehend.

A short while later the nurse appeared with what can only be described as an implement of torture. A bulky face mask with three strong, thick straps on it which was attached to the oxygen in the wall. It covered nan's mouth and nose. It worked with positive pressure, when nan breathed it helped her to inhale oxygen, but there had to be no air gap.

As soon as it was put on nan began thrashing around, trying to pull the monstrosity off of her face. It was heart rendering to watch, but this was absolutely our last chance saloon and I was not going to let it fail because nan tried to take it off every five minutes. The straps fastened securely around the back of her head and whilst it was virtually impossible to remove she was persistent to say the least.

After nearly an hour of her becoming increasingly distressed I asked the nurse to administer some drugs to calm her down, so that she could get the full benefit of the mask and the increased oxygen, and dutifully she went off to find a doctor. Ann had decided that night that she would sleep at my grandparents house to keep Grandad company and as we said goodnight and bade nan goodnight once she was calmer, I didn't realise that I would not see Ann again on good terms.

That night she and Grandad had a huge row over something as innocuous as a blind, which Ann had broken accidentally, and she flew off into a rage and drove back to Scotland without saying goodbye. I had had some insight into the messed-up psyche of Anne after our conversation, but still couldn't get to grips with how she could abandon her mum, such a gentle and sweet woman in her hour of need. I also realised that I was in no position to judge, given Anne's revelations to me and the fraught relationship that she had with her mother.

Anne left me her email and phone number and told me to keep her updated with how nan was, which I promised to do.

As the week progressed the mask seemed to be working and nan was able to spend some time without it on. She was lucid and frequently told me when I talked about getting her well enough to go home that she 'would not be going home again' and that ' she was going to die!'. I poo pooed it, but knew deep down that her life with my grandfather, with his cruel world and nasty temper was not something that she relished returning to.

But, still I refused to hear such poppy-cock and told her time and time again that she was on the mend and that the doctors were happy with her progress. Yet, still she insisted that she was going to die! I now realise that you can program our body to believe what ever it wants and that nan's fight had well and truly left her at this point. She actually wanted to die and sadly, I think willed it on as a blessed relief.

Chapter 37 Gone

On the Saturday, exactly one week after she had been admitted, I got to the hospital early and spent most of the day chatting and just sitting beside nan. Around 2pm I received a text from Charlie asking if I fancied a walk around our son's school fete. It was a pleasant afternoon, and I was feeling a little caged on the ward so agreed to be picked up for a while. I told nan that I was popping off and would be back later.

She didn't really hear me I don't think as she was sleeping, but I kissed her warm, soft cheek with its familiar smell and bade her goodbye for a while. It is at this point that I wish that I could turn back time and stop myself from going anywhere.

My biggest regret is leaving that ward and not bloody returning when I said I would! But, after an ice-cream with the kids and the promise of a catch up and a film with my family, who I had seen so little of all week, I went home instead of back to the ward, as I said I would!

Had I of gone back, I would have known that at around 8pm that night, as I was tucking into pizza and watching a film in the warm arms of my family that nan's breathing would get more laboured and over the next few hours she would become more and more unwell. My father apparently popped in from 5-6 pm and then crawled away because the alcohol was a calling, but she grew worse and worse alone in that bloody white, sterile bed!

Her breathing failed, her oxygen levels dropped like a stone and her heart rate increased. The doctor was called but didn't attend immediately, as he was busy seeing to other patients in a chronically over stretched department where he was expected to be in three places at once and do the work of six men!

Nan's notes, which I saw after her death show that he was called, and that by the time he came eventually at 02.10 she had passed away. No-one thought to tell the family to come and see her to say their goodbyes, to hold her hand and tell her as her light faded that she was desperately loved and always would be!

I settled in to a deep sleep at around 10pm and was nestled around the back of my husband when the phone rang abruptly at 02.35. I was up like a shot, adrenaline coursing through my body and making my knees shake and voice quiver as I answered a call from an unknown number.

'Mrs. Downey, can you get to the hospital safely?' A Philippino accented voice said quietly. 'Your grandfather is on his way too.'

'I'll be there in fifteen minutes' I said and hung up as I began trying to find the clothes I had thrown on the floor and not picked up last night, whilst brushing my teeth and trying to put my shoes on at the same time. It was like a bad dream, where all coordination leaves you and no matter how fast you are trying to move, it's like wading through treacle!

I was up and out in less than five minutes and flew the twelve miles into the hospital in a matter of minutes, racing my car around the bends at stupid speeds, given that my legs shook and my hands trembled the whole way. Thankfully there was not a thing on the road as I drove against the speed limit.

Please don't let her die, was my mantra the whole way. She must have just taken a turn for the worst I figured as I flung my car around the roads. I made it to the hospital in around thirteen minutes, swung my car into the first available space, right outside in a bay which was clearly marked disabled and set off to the main doors. I caught sight of my grandfather ambling through the foyer and rushed to catch him up.

'What do you think has happened?' He asked.

'I guess she's taken a turn for the worst, by the way the nurse asked us to come on back in' I counselled.

The ward was on the ground floor, in a maze of corridors, and without the hustle and bustle of the visitors and out patients the ward had an eerie silence about it.

The nurse was waiting for us as we walked up the ward, and I knew as we were ushered into the Matron's office that things were not good.

'Let me get you a cup of tea,' she kindly offered.

Grandad readily accepted, taking this ritual as a kindly gesture. Yet, I knew as a health professional that it was what we did before something awful happened. Create a social norm, some warm comfort as we broke bad news.

As calmly as I could muster, I asked quietly, ' she's gone hasn't she?' Before turning to face the nurse.

'I am afraid she died shortly after I called you' she explained.

I knew that this absolutely wasn't the case, they just wouldn't have wanted us to have driven whilst very upset, risking a crash on those lonely roads, in the dead of night.

' She went quietly' she consoled, 'Do you want to see her now?' She asked as she laid a kind hand on Grandads shoulder.

Time stopped in those few moments and I wanted to scream. My chest tightened and I tried to anchor my feet into the ground. I squeezed my eyes shut to stop the inevitable tears and knew that in true British 'Stoicism' that I wouldn't scream or cry loudly on the ward for fear of waking or upsetting other patients. How freaking admirable are we!!

Your world falls apart and you keep it in! At least that was the plan!

We walked behind the nurse, quietly and reluctantly. I held Grandads hand tightly and as we approached the four bedded bay where the curtains around nan's bed were drawn closed. The nurse ushered us through. There was nan, looking peaceful, with no sign of drips, monitors, oxygen, tucked up neatly in her bed.

She was cool to the touch and I knew at that point that she had not just bloody passed away, that she had died a good while before, had been certified as dead, not breathing anymore by a doctor, had been cleaned and laid out well before we got there. They let her die alone and in that fucking bed without her family.

I knew that it was not the time nor the place to start asking to see the notes. It was too late for that. My beautiful angel, my partner in crime, my friend and my angel was gone. Probably to a better place, but it was hard to rationalise that without soul sucking, heart wrenching grief.

I let Grandad say his goodbyes and tears rolled down my face, in an un-stoppable torrent as he gently kissed her forehead and held her hand, all the time speaking her name like a prayer. He was quite and composed, as was his way. It broke my heart. The nurse stayed with us and as he moved aside so that I could say my farewell the urge to fall on the bed next to her and will breath into those lungs just once more so that I could tell her to her face that she was loved, oh that she was more than loved, that she was adored and that her passing would forever leave a hole; no, a chasm in my life and that of my children.

I kissed her forehead, held her hand, stroked her face and hugged her as if my futile love would revive her. I soaked her shoulder in tears and felt my knees buckle as my chest heaved with silent crying. I told her all the reasons that I loved her, and thanked her for hours of laughter, for love, for support, for down right inappropriateness and for being a radiance of light in a dark, dark childhood. I have no idea how long I was there for. Maybe minutes, maybe many. Time was immaterial where death as concerned. It was final, and minutes no longer mattered.

When I could bear it no longer I turned and left the bay, moving silently through the curtains to find Grandad, who by now was regaling the nurse with his tales of hardship as a child.

I heard him say to the nurse, 'I'll get used to being on my own, had to fend for myself all my life, I'm used to hardship' it was full of self pity, with little grief. Maybe he was in shock, who knows?

Carrying her small bag of possessions in a yellow hospital bag we left the ward, armed with leaflets, forms and each other. There was a mountain of paperwork, notifications and endless organising to be done, and I knew that Grandad who by his own volition could barely fill in a cheque, would struggle making the calls and putting letters together, so I knew that I would be busy in the next few days. I also wanted to keep my father at arms length and away from organising anything. His habit of skimming money off the top and trying to rinse Grandad dry made me livid, and I felt like a warrior trying to keep the wolves from the door.

As we drove home it was around 4.30am and the dark clouds of night were beginning to break through into grey. It was still cold and silent as we rolled up onto the drive. In true British spirit the kettle went on, a true cure all and we sat mostly in silence, looking at the empty high back chair which was surrounded by nan's trinkets, her slippers and a cushion with 'Her Highness' written on. The strange thing with grief, is that suddenly you start to think you can feel the dead trying to communicate with you, to tell you that they are there, watching you as you sit trying to come to terms with their passing. I tried to feel if nan was there, tried to feel if she was standing next to me, yet nothing! Only her familiar 'nan' smell.

Grandad was desperate to tell people, to pick up the phone at 05.00 on Sunday morning. Thankfully, he listened to my voice of reason telling him that he could call everyone soon enough. I guess I wanted to hold onto the quiet memories in the house, and selfishly keep them just for me and him.

Anyone who knows me will know that I am not a natural sit still kind of person. I plan and do, and knew that the next few weeks, along with planning funerals, supporting Grandad and being a mum would be crazy. Grandad must have been on the same wave length as he began to root through nan's handbag. I wasn't sure what he was looking for as he delved deep into the small black leather bag, but a moment later he pulled out a small set of keys.

'Dand' (his pet name for me), 'go upstairs and in nan's wardrobe on the right hand side is a black tin. Bring it down will you.'

I did as I was bade, and whilst the black tin with a metal handle wasn't on the right, I found it nestled in amongst the clothes on the left, along with a large amount of metal Dinky toys, silver spoons and a multitude of other nick nacks my nan had collected over her lifetime. She was a fastidious collector of 'stuff', with a great eye for things worth money and rarity. Shutting the wardrobe I went back down stairs to where Grandad was sat on a high backed chair next to nan's empty one. Handing him the key I settled on to a small pine stool by his side to see what he thought was in the box.

The key turned easily and out fell twenty pound notes by the dozen! Grandad and I looked at each other in disbelief. ' What the hell?' I mused. ' Did she rob a bank?'

'It's her race tin' Grandad offered. 'I used to collect her winning's every day after she'd put her bet on. This is the money she won' I think. 'You count it,' he said pushing the overflowing tin at me.

My brain was fried with lack of sleep and grief, yet I sat on the floor and sorted the money into £100 piles. I counted out a whopping thirty piles totalling £3000. We were gob smacked. I had warned my grand parents about keeping large sums of money in the house, yet here it was, in all its glory, useless to nan now!

Grandad made a move to the oak wall cabinet with large doors on the bottom. Atop of it stood nan's trinkets, small ceramic animals, glass vases, pottery houses and all manner of 'clutter' as my grandfather called it. He opened the bottom door and came out holding a glass jar. ' count this too' he said, handing me the pot.

My eyes rolled and I laughed my socks off as I emptied out another £2000 in ten pound notes which my nan had hidden right next to my grandfather! Next, Grandad, who was by now on a mission sent me upstairs to get a small tin from the draw next to nan's bed. Inside lay around £300 in cash and three bank books. I handed them to Grandad, who handed them back for me to read. I read the entries, put down the books, gathered my thoughts and read them again, this time sharing what I read with Grandad.

Each book contacted a significant amount of money, yet the accounts had not been used for ten to fifteen years. One contained around £18000 and the other two around £13000 each. It was as if nan had forgotten that she had got them, as they had never been updated or used since the last deposit. Now, either my nan was a covert criminal, career gambler or had just saved this pot of money for a rainy day that never came, spending only her pension when she needed something! I showed the books to Grandad and told him that we would have to go to the banks at some point as what ever was Nan's had been passed on to him now.

I was worried that my father might come to find these large stashes of cash and so asked Grandad to put them some where safe until we could get to the bank! Grandad locked the money away and made towards the phone. It was, by now around 6 am and I felt it improper to hold him off calling anyone in our close family any longer.

He called Sue, my nan's sister first. I stood close by as he broke the news to her and my heart wrenched as I heard her scream out loud. Next came Anne, who with only a mobile number as a means of communication which was switched off I texted her and asked her to call home ASAP. Grandad didn't want to leave a voice mail. The last call was to my father. He answered the phone and told Grandad that he would be over shortly. I knew that my grandfather had left him till last given his penchant for large amounts of whiskey which would have left him probably still over the limit!!

I made Grandad yet more tea, some breakfast and pondered over the last few hours. My nan never ceased to amaze me. I wondered what other shocks she had in store for us! Grandad been talking about wanting to move to a little local town, which had some retirement flats in as soon as possible, given that winter was only a few months off.

I explained that there was lots to do to make that happen, but that I would help him all I could, handling the notifications, contacting and formalities. He went to get a wash in the upstairs bathroom and asked me to go through Nan's wardrobe to see what other secrets she had stashed in there. I function well under pressure and find that organising and sorting things out give a welcome break to the grief.

Before I could get round to this the back door opened and in walked my father. I made him a cup of tea and went back upstairs to sort the wardrobe as Grandad had asked. My father followed me up and seemed intent on helping me to 'sort things out'. Whilst I gently folded clothes, sorting out things that Grandad said could go to the Children's Hospice shop, as that was nan's chosen charity, my father rummaged through the other end of the wardrobe, through the small cupboard and into the bedside table. I tired my best to ignore him, but couldn't help but feel that he was up to no good and that his motives weren't helpful at all.

Hearing the front door go again I headed downstairs, feeling a bit numb and like the whole scenario was some sort of macabre sitcom show. My aunt had arrived and with it brought an air of noise and fuss to the house. Her and my grandfather didn't much care for each other and I tried to placate either side, just to keep the peace. I was making yet another cup of tea in the small kitchen, which backed onto the hall and back door when my father came through the hall door, heading out towards the back door carrying a large box. On the top of the box was a Silver spoon storage case and the metal Dinky toys, both of which I knew had come from nan's wardrobe.

I played dead, ignoring him as shamelessly he walked towards his car, which was parked opposite the house and loaded his loot, stolen from his mother who was barely cold into his car. I watched him again go off upstairs and come back down armed with another bag filled with my nan's collectables. This time there were thimbles, plant pots and china. He had thankfully not found the jewellery box which I had hidden under towels in the airing cupboard.

I didn't know whether to confront him, sound the alarm and make my grandfather aware at that point, or leave it until later once he had gone. I didn't want to make the day any worse than it was and frankly didn't want an altercation with this despicable human being. So, stupidly I did nothing. Hindsight, being the wonderful thing it is tells me now that I should have taken some photos of the back of his car loaded with goodies for future evidence, but I wasn't thinking like Miss Marple at that point. More fool me, I would come to realise in later weeks.

The day continued in the same fashion, with endless phone calls, endless visitors and endless cups of tea. I tried to hold it together, but broke down many times, as I found my favourite spoon, my favourite cup and such like tucked away the spare cup cupboard. I got out photo albums so that together we could reminisce and mentally begin packing away the house, as my grandfather told anyone who would listen that he didn't want to stay in the house but wanted to move as soon as was possible. I just wanted to make sure he was ok and that my father was kept as far out of the picture as possible.

While others chatted and talked about nan I began writing a list of things to do. It seemed endless and quite over whelming. It was made worse by my grandfather telling me that we should sort out as much a possible and get rid of the boxes of 'stuff' that my nan had lying around.

There were three boxes of Avon products in the small conservatory and I began sorting them out, asking my sister and sister in law and aunt what they wanted. I know that they thought that I was being mercenary and heartless, but in reality I wanted to get as much done as possible given that my husband was only going to be able to take a few days off work to look after the kids while I stayed to see Grandad was ok. I am hugely practical and efficient.

Perhaps in retrospect I should have just sat and drunk tea! My grandfather prattled on about hating nan's clutter and urged me to sort the pile of nan's paperwork which sat in the oak cupboard draw. Looking through I realised that it was going to take a significant amount of calls and letters in order to cancel catalogues, her Avon account, gardening subscription and such like.

Anne eventually rang the house phone and spoke with both me and my grandfather. She made it clear that she wasn't going to come down until the funeral, after her hasty exit before, and to be honest I was glad that she wasn't around. I had loved my grand mother with all my heart and it would have been hard to be around someone who was not upset about our loss.

After a long day spent around people who I wasn't entirely comfortable being with, I mentioned to Grandad about popping home to see the children and Charlie who I hadn't seen for over twenty four hours. He was not keen for me to go, and I felt immensely guilty, but I needed to just go and spend some time at home. I promised that I would be back first thing the following morning when the funeral director was due to come and we could begin to make plans for the funeral.

I drove home, mulling over what to do about my father blatantly taking my nan's things, probably to sell for money for Whiskey, and thought it best to speak with Charlie about it. He is like my voice of reason and is more logical than Dr Spock in Star Trek!!

Tucked up in my warm bed, nestled on my husband's chest I told him about my dad and his stealing. Charlie cussed me for not having taken a photograph, but was adamant that I should speak up as soon as possible and maybe tell my father that I knew what he had done! Was I up for orchestrating a train crash just twenty four hours after the death of my nan? I wasn't so sure!

That night I fell into an exhausted sleep. I've never struggled falling asleep , even when awful things have happened. It's like my brain, which functions at one hundred miles an hour shuts down completely to recharge then I wake up the following morning and bounce out of bed ready to go again. And, this is exactly what happened on the Monday morning. Bright and early I was back to Grandad's house ready to take on another day. I couldn't look at Nan's chair and found myself sniffing her pillow when I went into her bedroom as the grief and shock was tangible around me.

At 9am the Funeral Director called to make an appointment with us to discuss what was wanted for Nan's funeral. He was unable to come until the Tuesday so Grandad and I made arrangements to deposit the money which we had found into a bank account and I spent the morning on the phone working my way through lists of people to call to cancel mail, pay bills and tell them that my nan was no longer alive.

Some were genuinely saddened and empathetic, others merely gave me an address to write to so that accounts for bulbs and slacks, of which my nan appeared to buy many could be closed! It was a horrible job, marking the end of her life, in such a formal way. I had printed a pile of letters which could be sent and got Grandad to diligently sign each one. I was on auto pilot, just trying to do my very best to hold Grandad and myself together.

My father flitted in and out, searching through cupboards and shelves for loot. I could barely look at him and had to virtually bite my tongue in two to not scream at him about his blatant theft of my nan's possessions.

That afternoon Grandad came downstairs with Nan's jewellery box. When Nan was in hospital she had taken off her two small rings. I don't think that they were worth much, but sentimentally they meant everything to me. I had given one to my sister to wear at the hospital and I wore one too. Call them a bit of a talisman in order to keep nan safe and well. Fat lot of good it had done, now in those quieter moments I found that just holding it and twisting it round and round my finger that it really helped calm me down.

Nan had collected some pretty pieces of jewellery and I came upon a pretty ring in a bigger size which I suggested to Grandad that we could send up to Scotland for Anne to wear. I had found a few old school things of Anne's in cupboards and together with a lovely hand written card I posted them up to her, hoping that she would get some comfort from them.

How absolutely wrong was I! Two days later a text arrived into my inbox vehement in its manner and telling me that she hated me, did not want anything of nan's and that I had no right to send anything to her and that she never, ever wanted to see or hear from me again. I was shocked, devastated and utterly confused by her sudden animosity. Clearly something about my parcel had riled her and I concluded that something within the parcel had reminded her of her horrific experience and her reasons to hate Nan.

I didn't respond and told only Charlie of the text. We concluded that it was better at this point to ignore her. She clearly had a few issues!

Feeling once again isolated and alone, I sat that evening and wrote a long twelve page letter to my sister detailing my experiences at the hand of my dad and how much, despite a sad and desperate situation I had enjoyed having her in my life for the last week. I told her about my childhood and explained that I understood that while our experiences were like chalk and cheese, we didn't need to discuss these. It was personal, emotional and heart felt. I chose to drop it to her house early the following morning just after the school run. I was nervous, but hopeful that this might strengthen our relationship. Once again, I could not have called the next half hour and what proceeds after I knocked at the door.

Gingerly knocking, as it was only just gone 8am, I waited a while to see if she was in and going to answer the door. Just as I was about to post the wad of paper through the letter box the door snapped open and my sister stood at the door.

'I've come to give you something,' I said. 'I thought you might like to maybe read this'.

'You were always her favourite' she spat from nowhere. 'She gave you money and helped you so much with THOSE kids. And bought them school shoes.

I was gob smacked. She was right of course, my nan had helped me out with the six children, sometimes throwing me a twenty pound note towards school shoes, which used to cost us for six pairs, three times a year around four hundred pounds a time! It was the one thing that I refused to compromise on and always bought the kids leather, fitted shoes that cost the earth!

She bought all six presents and would often send me home with a tin of beans and some tined peaches, but I didn't perceive it to be that I was her favourite, just that I was the only one with children at that point and that she as Great-Grandma wanted to help them out. It was nothing less than she would have done for my sister's children, had she had any!

The torrent of abuse and ranting continued, tearing me apart, slating my children and my husband. I tried to interject and explain that nan and I were closer because I didn't have a relationship so to speak with my mother or father, and that my grand parent's more or less raised me, but my words fell on deaf ears. I didn't have the strength to scream back, to rant on about unfairness, about her mother's despicable treatment of me or the fact that I was the victim of abuse. No, I stood there and took it. Tears rolled down my face once again and my knees shook. My sister vented her wrath until she was done, then while staring me in the eye turned on her heel and slammed the door.

I stood there shell shocked, wondering if anyone else in the street had heard the furore and staring like an eegit at my letter, so full of love and explanations. When my legs stopped shaking enough for me to walk I headed for my car. In auto pilot I moved it down the street before calling my mother hysterical. She was matter of fact, telling me that they were all mad and that I was better off without them in my life! I know now with the wonder of hind sight the what she said is absolutely true, but back then, with my heart wrenched with grief I just felt even more alone.

It was going to be tough getting through the days between then and the funeral with my family frequenting the house so often. I decided to just stay out of the way! That proved difficult when a few days later my father decided that he wanted to come to the bank, in a nearby village in order to close nan's accounts and transfer the monies over to Grandad. I refused to drive with him in my car, sharing the same air and so we arranged to meet him there.

The bank manager was empathetic and listened as Grandad told him about his marriage and childhood. As he chatted the manager updated nan's bank books. I was gob smacked when he totalled them up to come to around 27k! This was on top of the large amount of cash we had found. There was still one bank to go to in order to close the account and Grandad wondered where nan had managed to get the best part of 30k from without him knowing!

The last bank account contained around 14k. That was some gaming or saving habit that my nan had! I made sure that Grandad put the money into his savings account which was accessed by a bank book. I did not trust my father to root out a cash card and begin drawing money!

As my grandfather sorted the transaction, my father began wittering on about his ongoing car troubles. On and on he went until my grandfather offered him 3k in cash to go and sort out his car. My father had gambled well, knowing that his father would be feeling generous having just come into such a large amount of cash. He piled the £20 notes into his pocket greedily with little thanks.

The funeral was set for ten days after nan had died. My sister wanted to arrange the wake and I was happy to let her and Anne arrange every thing. My focus for the day was getting Grandad through the day with minimal upset from my father or Anne.

The day of the funeral was crisp and blue, with bright flowers that bounced in the gentle breeze. I had sorted out the younger children and asked my mum and aunt to come and be my army at the funeral. I felt slightly intimidated being hated by so many people and I needed to feel that someone had my back, should the shite hit the proverbial fan! Charlie was going to be busy with the older children, all who wanted to come and pay their last respects.

As the hearse and cars drew up outside the house my heart broke in two again. I walked up to the hearse and traced the flowers that lay in the window with my finger and struggled to believe that the body of my nan was actually in the car! I am sure that most of us have had a surreal moment at a loved ones funeral, where we think they will suddenly walk in to the room and profess that its been a bad joke on their behalf. However, no such luck on this sad day.

We had made sure that there was enough room in the two cars for immediate family, with partners travelling in their own cars the short journey down to the church where my nan and Grandad had married sixty years before. As I backed away from the hearse to take my place in the cortege I noticed both doors closed.

The cars were both full, with my sister's partner and brother's girlfriend taking my space. The footman looked confused as I walked towards the car and then turned back, incredulous at the gall of the people I shared blood with. Neighbours and friends watched as I slipped back, head held high to Charlie and my sister looked sheepish. 'Bastards' I muttered under my breath to Charlie, determined to not give them the satisfaction of seeing me upset.

Instead we drove as a family to the church, and I caught up outside the church with Grandad, who seeing me, offered me his arm to walk directly behind the coffin as it began the walk to the church. My brother's, father and the pall bearers walked in front of us and I tried my best to control my breathing to stop me from breaking down. Instead I focused on Grandad, and the large white wreath on the top of the coffin.

The service was personal, by a vicar who knew our family and was well planned by my sister. I was happy to let her have free rein over the ceremony as I opted to sort practical things. Nan's favourite songs and hymns were played, as we bent our heads for the prayer a large bumble bee buzzed by me, stopped and then headed for the coffin where it rested until it moved ready for the burial. I know that this was nan, showing her presence in nature and felt better for this knowledge, crazy as it may have sounded. As the coffin was carried out of the church to the tune of We'll Meet Again by Vera Lynn I finally allowed myself to sob. Noisily I moaned as Grandad and I followed the coffin out into the bright sunshine.

Burials are just mad aren't they? Committing the body of the one that you love to a cold and wet, freshly dug hole in the ground. I think I would rather have a viking funeral pyre! We threw the per-functionary dirt onto the coffin and a rose onto the coffin too. As others headed off to the wake in the church hall I struggled to make my legs work. Dressed in heels and a dress I found myself sunk by the graveside, blithering like an idiot. I felt people around me but was unable to speak or react to their concerned comments.

I felt an arm around my shoulders and realised that it was my father who had slunk up to me. As my stomach churned at his touch, on my other side I heard the dulcet tones of my mother saying 'I'll handle this' as she shooed him away, all the time resisting the temptation to place him in the grave besides my Nan!

As a family we didn't stay at the wake for long. My sister, stepmother and Anne seemed petrified of my aunt and mum and did not want to put a foot wrong, for fear that my mother's ferocious temper may hunt them down. I felt safer and protected by the barrier that the strong women in my life and my husband gave me. I spoke to family friends, many of whom I had not seen for many years who told me how proud nan had been of me and the kids.

When we had stayed for a perceived 'right' amount of time we slunk away, only saying a goodbye to Grandad. My sister looked perplexed as to why we had not spoken. I am unsure whether it was because she has a dreadful memory and had forgotten the venomous things that she had said a week previously, or whether she wanted us to move forward. Again, another thing that I may just not know.

Post funeral life was strange. I visited the grave every day for a month, until we went on holiday and some days I took Grandad there too. We picked fresh flowers from nan's garden and filled the sinking grave with colour. I placed a windmill and owl on the grave that the children chose and spent many hours on a bench, eyes wet talking to nan. The grief was all encompassing and exhausting.

I managed to avoid my father at the house and when asked by Grandad what had happened to the items that were in the wardrobe, I finally told him about my father stealing them and being seen selling the toys at the Toy Fayre the weekend after nan died. Grandad was shocked and mentioned it to my father the next time he saw him. My father by all accounts fervently denied the accusation. I hadn't expected anything less. At least now he knew, that I knew, exactly what he had done and that I was not going to be frightened into silence any more.

In days where my loneliness and grief left me feeling alone and aghast I focused once again on the beauty all around me, the love and strength that I gained from my children and husband and the love that I held for my grandmother. If you have been bereaved then take each day one moment at a time. Accept that grief is inevitable and that the days pass anyway. It's ok to feel low, sad, to want to scream and shout and lament loudly. This is normal. Although you may feel that your heart may feel empty and broken. All of these things are absolutely OK.

In the months after my nans funeral I managed to avoid my father and the rest of the family. I would pop over most mornings straight from the school run. Sometimes I would run to the grave with a few flowers or just to go and chat to nan before I headed for Grandad's house. I knew that my father would not venture out that early, given that he spent every night in a bucket, obliterated from his whiskey habit! He knew better than to knowingly drink and drive.

Around three months after my nan's death I got a call from my grandfather sounding concerned. My father had told him that he was coming to the house to begin to move some furniture and items from the house and Grandad didn't know how to stop him. I phoned my father on his mobile and it became quickly apparent that he was drunk and at a Sunday night BBQ at maybe my brother's house.

'Martyn, Grandad has told me that you are wanting to go and move some items from the house. He's worried and not wanting you to touch anything. I am warning you not to touch a thing. Do you under stand me?' I quietly said.

I had put the phone at that point on loud speaker and was in a way so grateful that I had done so and that my children were not witness to the profanities and hatred that fell from my father's mouth as he replied, 'You fucking cunt, fucking bitch. Who do you think you are? I'll make sure that you get nothing, no money, nothing, you whore!'

Before I could respond Charlie had crossed the kitchen, taken the phone from my hand and calmly said 'Enough, you will not speak to my wife like that and you will not be taking anything from Joe's house, do you understand me?'

The line went silent and then dead. Clearly my father did not want a confrontation with my six foot, well built husband. Charlie was the 'quiet one', mild mannered until it was necessary to reach a flash point. The bully in my father only wanted to insult and seek to frighten those he thought were weaker than him. How wrong he was and how he had under estimated me so much.

Knees knocking with adrenaline we drove over to Grandad's to support him if my father appeared. It wasn't long before we heard the side door open and Charlie, quick as a flash went to meet my father. There was no loud raising of voices, it wasn't necessary, but Charlie, being a lot taller than my father, and without all the bullshit and bravado merely told him that 'nothing, absolutely noting would be leaving the house, unless Joe asked for items to go'.

By all accounts my father merely whimpered in agreement and slunk off to the bathroom while we made a jubilant exit. I felt stronger than I had done in years and wanted to embrace the new found empowerment. I was never going to allow myself to be bullied ever again.

Life moved on again. Christmas hit us like a train and the New Year followed. My little family and I were happy, settled and very grateful for our life.

Chapter 38 'Truth Will Out'

It was a freezing cold February afternoon. A Wednesday I believe. I was by now a woman, early forties, struggling with the scars from a past which haunted me daily back then. I was mum to six beautiful children, yet life although stressful was fringed with the beauty that having children in your life brings to you.

Once again car had broken down and I was coatless, penniless and carless, in a shrine to St Mary Magdalene, waiting on a bench for my car to be fixed. I had no cash for a coffee in the cafe over the road and so sat contemplating life in the icy wind which cut through my thin jumper like a knife. I was out of my mind with worry and had to cry in the garage, real tears in order to ask the lovely men, who knew me well to mend my car and accept payment on payday, at the end of the month. Unable to say no, they had thankfully agreed and now I bided my time in the church yard, willing them to hurry up.

There were arrangements to be sorted regarding the Grandparents day at Loola's school the following day and I took the opportunity to call my mother, given that I had little else to do whilst freezing my nuts off, in a church yard!

Deep in my heart I knew that our relationship was doomed. She spent as little time with me as possible, especially the revelations about my father trying to abuse me, Bong and the confirmed abuse of his sister by my father. She had not wanted to discuss it, and had point blank told me that she would not give credence to my allegations with her testimony of my father's abusive assaults on her.

The phone rang and I got the familiar dread in my stomach. It was me that made most contact just to try and cling onto the crumbling relationship and keep some kind of string attached to her. I was desperate and despondent from the outset as we began to chat about whether or not she was able to come to the proposed Grandparents day and what the logistics may be. Loola had been desperate for her to come, especially when all of her friends had their kindly, loving grandparents attending. I had broached the subject with her a few weeks before and she had tentatively agreed that it should be 'fine' but wouldn't commit to details at that point.

That day she didn't sound particularly enthused by the prospect and when asked if she wanted to stay at our house, so that all six of her grandchildren could see her on her short trip to the hills, she declined, telling me that she wanted to come up and down in one day. I felt myself stiffen at the rejection once again and those feelings of despondency once again cloaked my psyche. I felt so sad that my children, all six who were innocent and desperate to feel loved too would once more miss out, because of the issues that she had with me.

I braved a small challenge in an attempt to change the situation around so that I might be able to spend a bit more time, one to one with my mum. She was not having a jot of it, making up excuse, after excuse about why she couldn't come up the night before, stay after the event or spend a bit more time with me, and my children.

Frozen to the core and becoming more than a little bit upset, I braved a 'anyone would think you didn't want to spend time with me!' Those words were uttered and there was no rewinding or taking them back. That's it, I had said it, thrown her a line to finally give me an answer. Like the proverbial truth drug, it was done. Nothing could have prepared me for what was said next.

There was silence, and you could have heard a pin drop on the line as we both waited for the next line.

'I find you difficult to be around' she spat. 'You're prickly and put me under pressure when I come up to the area to spend time with you, that's why I don't tell you when I'm coming up'.

Time stopped and I felt myself inwardly deflate and collapse. My legs buckled and I collapsed into the small circle of stones around the serene looking Virgin Mary who seemed to not mind the freezing cold sleet and bitterly cold wind.

I struggled to breathe and began to shake. It was what I had always known. I made her feel uncomfortable and ill at ease, just because I wanted her to behave like a mum to me and a grandmother to my children. In merely asking her for a few hours of her time when she came to the area visiting my aunt or her brother this was construed as being needy and pressurising her.

Breath returning and wanting answers now, I pushed her further, almost goading her into telling me finally the truth. I challenged her, my bat-fink wings well and truly made of steel and protecting me from the inevitable revelations which I knew would follow.

'You treat me differently from the others and always have' I tried to explain, wanting her to apologise and admit to herself and me that she knew that she did this.

'It's because I don't love you like I love the others' she responded, 'it's different and you need to accept that!'

That was it, the deed was done, and those words could never be retracted, they were etched on my memory and my heart forever and a day. However, I bizarrely felt elated. I felt lighter and thankful that she had set me free. That I finally knew that it wasn't really me, but the fact that she didn't love me like my siblings which had left me feeling so different for all those years.

 As I shook with cold, feeling the sleet in my hair I gazed at the statue of the Virgin Mary, in the tiny shrine and felt more at peace and at one with her serenity. I thanked my mother for her frank counsel and calmly said 'Thank you for that, it's made it all so much clearer and I know exactly where we stand with each other now' and calmly ended the call.

I was aware of a gentle mewing sound as I sank to my knees on the hard, frozen concrete step, now sprinkled with dusting of snow. That soft whimpering was me. Unable to speak or hold onto my broken heart, I made only sound that I could. Shaking with the cold, and I suspect shock I tried to compose myself. The shrine was next to a main road and there were passer's by strolling briskly up the road, going about their business. I must have looked quite a spectacle, small redhead, ill equipped for the biting wind and sleet, sobbing noisily in a Catholic shrine on a Wednesday afternoon.

For a time I was unable to summon the strength to get up and move. The cold wind bit into my face and had the tears not been salty they would have frozen in rivers down my face. I had never felt so absolutely alone and abandoned and almost ready to quit. What had I done to deserve parents who really couldn't act as such? Once again the quote ' The sins of the fathers' came rushing to my mind as I tried to calm myself down enough to go and reclaim my car and collect my children from school. If only my mother's experiences with her own mother had been different, maybe she could have loved me more? Maybe if I hadn't challenged the status quo and decided to fight back she would have loved me more, so many what ifs.

Slouched over against the wind I made my way to the garage to collect the car. I knew the mechanics well, given that my old banger of a car was a frequent visitor in their premises once a month at least and they looked concerned when the usually jovial, smiley Dani burst in, unable to speak for tears and snot to pay a paltry £50 toward a £500 bill. They didn't make eye contact as I put the £50 on my maxed out credit card and took the keys, knowing that I didn't dare speak for fear that I would become hysterical in such a male dominated environment.

I was tight for time and didn't want to risk being late to collect my son from school, so put my foot down in my now functional car. It was hard to concentrate on the road given that my head felt like it was going to explode, and how I did not collide with another vehicle I really do not know.

Chapter 39 True Grit

In true Dan style I began to calm down enough to not alarm my seven year old son in the playground. I have a huge amount of resilience and the ability to look absolutely fine and dandy, even when the world collapses around me.

Resilience is something that I have spent much time studying. It intrigued me why I was able to go through so much, yet still be fairly functional, some might say 'functioning mad' and live a life filled with joy, happiness and success.

The dictionary definition describes resilience as 'the capacity to recover quickly from difficulties, toughness'

It's the ability of some individuals to face hardship and challenges, yet still bounce back stronger than ever. Psychologists know that there are a couple of fundamental factors involved in developing resilience and I know that I have them in abundance. They are a positive attitude, optimism and the ability to see failure as useful in order to help them learn.

From an early age I was able to see the positive in most situations, knowing instinctively that where I was was not where I had to stay. I realised that if my world was to turn out differently from how it was when I was born I needed to be a good student, get a good education and keep paddling against the proverbial tide which sought to keep me near the shore. And that is what I did. With every trial and tribulation sent to try me, I worked out a way to change the outcome and get me nearer to where I wanted to be. I kept good company with friends and my children and loved having them in my life. A good network is crucial to having resilience.

Normally, I allowed myself minimal whine time and developed the ability to pick myself up, dust myself off and move off again with impeccable speed. Yet, on that day I didn't honesty know how I was going to move on from the hurt and anger I felt towards the situation with both of my parents. For the first time in my life I felt weak and needy and clung to my husband like I needed him for breath. He was then and has always been my rock and stability. I think it truly shocked him at just how broken and beaten I was that night, as he held me tight as I wept, wept and wept some more.

How is it that tears can be endless? I should have been a dehydrated, wrinkled prune with the amount of water that I leaked! I fell straight to sleep with sore and swollen eyes and woke up with the numb realisation that comes with the feeling of grief after a bereavement.

That day we had to attend the grandparent's assembly at Loola's school, which had been the route of the phone call with my mother the day before. Little, broken sleepyhead left me feeling raw, emotional and incredibly sad. I had told my older children when they saw me upset, that I now knew why my mother treated me so differently, that I was hurt

210

beyond belief, but that I would be ok. I think because I didn't try and hide my grief from them they coped much better with the broken shell of their usually strong as iron mother.

With the younger children Loola and Zoom, I told them that mummy was sad, but that she was ok. They took this at face value and offered me sweets and a hug. What a cure all! In situations like this I have a tendency to want to open a bottle of alcohol and get blind drunk as quickly as I can.

Having grown up with an alcoholic father, I deliberately avoided using alcohol as a crux, knowing that with the amount of stress I had had in my life, that I could well have become alcohol dependent in a heartbeat. So instead of a large glass of Chardonnay, I wept into my decaf tea!! How bloody well rock and roll!

So, husband in tow we trotted off to the assembly at the school which resembled Hogwarts. A beautiful building, filled with gleaming teachers and happy students, the hall was filled with joyous grandparents and their children all watching their young charges sing and dance on the stage.

As I looked around I felt the tears begin to roll down my face once more and I had to bite my lip hard to not openly sob.

The way that the grandmothers looked at their daughters and their grand-daughter's filled me with sorrow at what Loola and I did not have with my mother. I wept for the years that had gone by where I so desired to be loved and cherished, yet more often that not, felt like a let-down, a failure and a cuckoo in the nest.

In order to not let Loola see me openly sobbing, I left the hall and staggered into the hall, closely followed by a kind looking teacher, who not even knowing my name gave me a warm hug and tried to make me feel better. The kindness of strangers throws me sometimes. I maintain that most people are good and filled with beauty.

I was so grateful to her for such an open display of empathy, and as the tears slid once again down my face I knew that I had enough good people around me that it would all be ok.

Chapter 40 On The Mend

The days turned into weeks and I felt myself get stronger, bit by bit. In a way I felt a little grateful to my mum for freeing me from the unhealthy cycle I was in.

Trying to get her to love me just a little bit more and in different way than she was able to do was fruitless, demanding and futile. She could not love me more and manufacture something that was not there, no more than I could pretend to love someone I did not love.

You see, for all of our differences, we are immensely similar in so many ways. We both wear our hearts on our sleeves, are feisty and have a way of always wanting to protect the underdog, that is unless she is your daughter!

I had called my mum every few weeks for a chat, so that she didn't forget me and sent her a text on a regular basis. More often than not she didn't respond to my texts and I was left again feeling dejected and unwanted again.

She had proclaimed in our last ever call that the reason that she didn't call me was because she didn't know what to say and was always worried that I might overreact if I found about something that had gone on in Wales that we hadn't been invited to.

I guess she had something in that observation. If she told me about a large, fun and yummy family dinner or BBQ that was held for my siblings, their partners and grandchildren that we weren't invited to, I did used to get that familiar punch in the gut that I associated with disappointment. She really could not understand why I would be so sad and upset that me and my family were always an after-thought or not even a thought at all.

As the weeks passed by I remained sad and cried in those warm moments of silence. Certain songs had to be turned off and the film Brave was something I couldn't be in the room to watch.

The complex relationship between the main character and her mother resembled my own too closely and I found myself sobbing hysterically! I went back to work and had so much support within my team. Between them, friends and my gorgeous family I began to heal, at least to the outside world. I was back to functioning and life moved on.

Chapter 41 Sins of the Fathers

A few months had gone by since my divorce from my mother. She had not attempted to call, apologise or offer an olive branch and I was learning to live without her and my large extended family in my life. There was no question of my siblings maintaining contact with me, and so the only family member I spoke with was my aunt-mother.

The Spring was well and truly under way and Easter had been and gone in a blur of chocolate eggs and badly worded clues after our annual Easter Egg Hunt! My kids love the rituals around occasions and they have developed traditions for Christmas, Easter and New Year.

One Sunday morning I was sat having a cup of tea in the kitchen, appreciating the ever-changing view out of the large picture window when Bong walked into the kitchen looking tearful and upset.

'I need to tell you something, mum' he said.

'Sure thing, Bong. Are you gay?' I chuckled. 'You know it's not an issue for us if you were' I continued, giving him a squeeze. Our daughter Min had come out to us a few years before and it wasn't a big deal whatsoever.

'No mum' he said in a choked voice 'Grandy tried to touch me, and I didn't know how to tell you.'

You could have heard a pin drop in the kitchen as I held him close as he cried and as I came to terms with the words that he had held onto for four long years.

'I'm so sorry Bong' was all I could say as the tears fell down my face into his hair.

I asked his permission to talk about it and asked him when and where this had happened. There was never any question about whether I believed him. From my work with safeguarding children I knew that they didn't make this kind of stuff up and that for him to have told this to me would have taken a huge amount of courage. I also knew because of the revelations from my aunt about what my father had done to her, what he had done to me and to my mother that every word of what Bong was saying was true.

I let him talk and told him that it was not his fault and that he was not to blame.

At the point where the conversation drew to a natural silence I asked him what he would like to happen. I explained that we would have to tell the police in order to make sure that my father's youngest grandchild was safeguarded and that going to the police would spark up a Children's Services referral. I reassured Bong that there was counselling available to him and that he did not have to pursue the matter through the courts if he did not want to.

His bravery dumfounded me and called into question my own cowardice in never having the guts to report the crimes he committed to the police. There had not been a day gone by in the last five years when I hadn't wished that I was brave enough to go to the police station and report him.

My knowledge of the court system and the way that it treated victims of sexual abuse and rape, had made me quite loathe to put myself out to the sharks and have every aspect of my life investigated whilst a case was built. I had taken anti-depressants for a few months and knew that with this and my sexual abuse counselling that this may make me an unreliable witness.

My mother had stated that she would never collaborate my abuse with her own, and I knew that my aunt would fervently deny what she had told me as my nan laid dying in the hospital. Yet, in the light of these horrific revelations I knew that we had no choice but to inform the police.

With a shaking hand, I ushered Bong out of the room and dialled 101. As the call handler answered the call I began to explain exactly what had occurred that morning, bringing into the mix my mother's, my own and my aunt's abuse at the hands of this sexual predator.

My voice choked up as I described the encounters of my son, taken to a rugby match by my father, who tried to touch him up in the cubicle when bong went to pee. I had worked out that my son was around ten years old when this happened and I knew that he had carried this around with him for four years, not knowing the significance of the actions of this abhorrent man or maybe that it was so wrong back then.

I had thought that I was protecting my children by moving fifteen miles away from where my father lived. I had caught the looks of appreciation as he scanned my growing girls, up and down. I couldn't pinpoint back then, just why this made me so uncomfortable, as I hadn't began to have the flashbacks at this point, my intuition just told me that there was something malevolent and sordid about his wandering eyes. I had assumed that he was only interested in girls!

How wrong was I? I explained to the officer that I had, had little or no contact with my father and had actively sought to protect the children from him, but had failed, I admitted with a screaming heart.

She took the details and advised that a Children's Services referral would be generated and this would set the whole Safeguarding wagon into motion. A police officer would be in touch she told me and both Bong and I would be need to be spoken to.

My worst nightmare had indeed come true with my father trying to lay his filthy hands upon my children, and having Children's Services involved in our family. Even to a rational professional person, Children's Services set my heart racing at their power and influence, having worked alongside them in the court and domestic abuse arena for many years.

The die was cast and we would need all of our strength to get through these challenges. Given that it was a Sunday morning I knew that nothing much would happen that afternoon and braced myself for what my Monday would hold.

I spoke with Bong about the 'what happens next' and told him that I would be beside him all the way. I leant on my husband emotionally and cried once again for hours, out of sight of the children, for what was my childhood and for the distress and angst created because of this monster. I wanted him dead. There is no easy way to say this, or any euphemism needed, because I wanted the bastard, un-breathing, unconditionally without life, DEAD.

I took my keys that evening from the shelf and decided that I was going to go and kill him so that he couldn't ever inflict harm on anyone else. I figured that if I waited long enough outside the house I could run him over, quickly and easily, job done. I didn't care how long I had to wait for the moment to come, that patience would prevail and I would finally rid the earth of his foulness forever.

I hadn't accounted for my husband's astuteness at that point however. As he asked me where I was going, I was unable to lie and filled with venom, in a calm, matter of fact voice I told him that I was going to kill my father. The look of horror on his face registered with me, that he might just have a problem with this activity, but I held fast as tears rolled down my face.

'Dan, you can't kill him,' he reasoned

'I can, I'm going to run him over' I countered, no justification needed in my mind.

'Give me your keys, please' he asked gently.

'No' I stubbornly said, having not thought about Mr Rational and his fucking logic, and the fact he might not support me in this course of action.

'I thought you had my back and would want that bastard dead' I began to sob.

Taking me in his arms and holding me tight was all I needed to drop the keys, giving him enough time to confiscate them. I sobbed retched tears once again and felt weak. Fucking weak, for the first time in many, many years.

'You would go to prison if you killed him, you know that' Mr Rational reasoned, 'and what would happen to the children then?'.

I knew he was right and that his logic was important, however in my heart, I wanted to be the one to stop this once and for all, to get payback for all the people that he hurt and all the pain he had caused. That it was my right. I was a mother lion, willing to die for my children, passionately protective over them and I had failed one of them. My desire to make good the situation and tear him limb from limb was inherent, and not one I felt I could easily control.

The night passed with me falling into an exhausted sleep on Charlie's lap and dreaming crazy, violent dreams. I awoke to a feeling of foreboding and impending doom as I knew that I would get a call from a social worker first thing, and probably the police too.

I was desperate to call my mother, knowing that she would thrive on the drama and my neediness, yet I held fast, preferring to share what was going on the chosen few friends who I knew would not judge. I know she would have been there for me, but I needed her to be there for me on an every day basis, and not just in a crisis.

Bong wanted to go to school and seemed fine so went off, leaving Charlie and I to fire fight. Thankfully, I didn't have to wait too long for a call from a pleasant sounding social worker, who introduced herself as Natalie. I was naturally hostile as she chatted about what had happened and arranged an appointment to come later that afternoon to meet with me. I put myself for the first time in my clients's shoes.

Children's Services put the fear of God into my client's and I was no different. Were they going to take my children away? Would they say I was totally nuts, crazy, mad and have me removed from my house? So many negative thoughts crowded my mind as I tried to preoccupy myself with more pleasant thoughts!

Sometime after lunch she arrived, casually dressed, with little pomp and circumstance and over a cup of tea, wanted to chat about the revelations and moreover my past. She wanted the minute details about my whole family, their families and my relationships with siblings, my mother, father and the abuse that my father had perpetrated against so many people. She began to write down a family tree in her neat script and asked me in turn about any abuse or my relationship with each and every one.

At each revelation of abuse, she sighed, and I once again sobbed, as I told her about my flashbacks, which started around 2011, about being abused by two other perverts, about trying to protect my children and about the fractured relationships all around me.

As I gave her details of my father's sick trail of abuse through the years, she looked at me seriously.

 'This type of abuse if often inter-generational and has touched many people' she said. 'in families with domestic abuse, sexual abuse, poverty and alcohol abuse, Children's Services are often involved much more, you all seem to have flown well below the radar' she offered out, incredulously.

Seeing the whole, disgusting, tangled and debauched web put down on paper broke my heart. I had always set out to be the best parent I could be, had wanted to be a good example of a sound and fair parent to my children, despite all the back story. I was petrified that this social worker with all her power and influence, might find a way to take my children off me.

Perhaps she might think I was bonkers and incapable as a parent, that my damage and issues might prohibit me from parenting anymore........so many uncertainties, which I wanted answering 'right now', yet I knew that anything to do with the Police and Children's Services took endless time, and this was something that would be in our lives for a good while, as a minimum.

Three hours later Natalie concluded that in order to safeguard my children there would be a Strategy meeting held the following morning. For those of you not in the know, a Strat. (Strategy Meeting) happens when concerns have been raised about the safety of a child or children.

During the meeting, professionals, such as the Police, Teachers, Social Workers, Mental Health team etc. convene and discuss whether more formal proceedings are going to follow, such as a Section 47 (child protection assessment) or a Section 17 (child in need assessment) need to be instructed.

These are both huge assessments and last many months. I had known from the outset that I needed to be seen to be protecting the children from further harm. I am not sure if murder was factored into the protection of the children, but wasn't about to share my previous night's plans with the Natalie!!

Chapter 42 A Walk In Their Shoe's

In my day job as an Independent Domestic Violence Advisor (IDVA) I attended these so called Strat. meetings and was horrified that here I was, on the other side of the fence, being judged and talked about by another group of professionals who thought that they knew my family. I felt seriously out of control and out of my depth.

Natalie volunteered that she had spoken to a police officer that morning called Julie, who was going to be calling to see both me and Bong the following afternoon. Natalie had mentioned that the police felt that my brother, Leo who was the only person with a child in the family that had direct contact with my dad should be made aware of the allegations against him in order to safeguard his young son.

I made it known that because I thought my father was only interested in girls, at the birth of my nephew the year before I had decided to not tell my brother anything as I did not feel that it was relevant to him, and certainly did not want to upset him and harm my tentative relationship with him and his wife.

Yet, I knew that if the police phoned him, or went out to pay him a visit on my behalf it would rock the boat much more than if I told him myself. It was my tale to tell and I felt that I could back it up with my experience, and that of my mother's and aunts to help him understand just what a danger my father posed to his one year old son. I thought that this would all end in a much more positive way! Clearly the Gods of good endings were not looking down on me that night!

That evening, I sat on the bed in my room and dialled the number for him. His wife answered. We had got on well, and although they both accepted that I did not go to their wedding for some reasons concerning my relationship with our father, they had no idea what was coming. In retrospect, I now know that had I allowed the police to go out and speak with them things may have turned out differently.

However, I did what I thought was best for everyone at the time and I made a call there and then to tell her first, as if Leo got off the phone very upset, as I suspected he would I wanted her to be able to support him.

So, in a few words I informed her about what had been disclosed by Bong, what had happened that day and made her aware that the police had asked me to call. There was silence on the other end of the phone as she handed the phone to Leo, who by now, must have known something was very wrong by her quiet and shocked silence.

 I couldn't face idle chit chat with Leo and with tears streaming down my face I began to take Leo through the events of the last five years, detailing the abusive behaviour of our father towards so many people, and culminating in the present day with Bong's disclosure. I briefly mentioned my mum and my aunt and then I ended with the dilemma that I faced, of having the police tell me that they were going to go to his house to help safeguard the baby, or inviting me the choice to tell him myself. I told him that I thought that I owed it to him and his family to hear it first from me.

He began to cry as I went through the story and at the end just said 'ok' and hung up. I was shocked and bemused by his actions, yet knew that he was close to my father and must be extremely shocked by the contents of my call. I sent him a text and told him that I would speak to him in the week and that I loved them all loads.

There was no response, yet I didn't mind. My mind whirring with the enormity of what I had just disclosed to my poor brother. Yet knew that there would be more fall out from my father's reign of perversion.

The following day, a Tuesday the police came to speak to me before they saw Bong after school. They asked me about the events of my childhood, what I knew about my father's assaults on others and if I would make a statement, formally allowing them to pull my father in for questioning.

Feeling a failure again and so incredibly weak, I told them that I couldn't make a statement and report anything formally. I was petrified of the court system and how I may be painted out to a jury. She knew what my job entailed and that I had had first hand experience of witnessing my clients in the witness stand and agreed with me when I said that now just wasn't the right time to make a formal complaint to the police.

I felt less crazy, having disclosed historic abuse, especially in the light of the Saville enquiry, yet knew that with no physical evidence, a scanty time line and no corroboration from my aunt, my mother or Bong, my case was destined to fall flat. I think Julie got that, but had hoped to be able to lock up this paedophile for good.

She asked for consent to speak with Bong, who by now was back from school and I gingerly waited in the lounge while they chatted.

During the chat I took the time to send a text to Leo to check that he was ok. Short, simple,

I love you so much and hope you are ok.

There was little more that I could say at that point in time.

The kitchen door opened some twenty minutes later and Bong came out, looking relieved.

'Can we have a quick chat' Julie, the Child Protection Officer asked.

We three, sat down at the kitchen table where on she began to tell me that Bong didn't want to make a formal statement, and asked me how I felt about that. I countered that I completely supported his decision, given my line of work with the police and courts, that it had made me quite jaded with the conduct of the court system in prosecution cases. I couldn't bear to have to sit and listen to my son's allegations been torn apart by a barrister for the defence.

I desperately did not want the social worker to think that I was not safeguarding Bong, or any of the other five children. I knew that not safeguarding your children might mean that they are removed from your care, I had seen many mothers lose their children after refusing to safeguard them from perpetrators, and I was not going to let this happen to my precious children. I would dance to whatever tune Children's Services wanted in order to maintain stability for the children and keep them with me.

I have to admit, both Julie and Natalie were respectful of the decision Bong had made. However, they both felt that I should make a formal statement to the police to enable them to question and, possibly prosecute my father. My head, not in a fit state to be logical told me that it was not a good path to pursue.

I rationalised that being hated by most members of my father's side of the family, after a hate campaign started by my father following the death of my nan, three years previously had left me with many haters, who would come out and support my father. He had tried to slander my name at every point and I could not see without the endorsement of my mother and aunt how a case would ever be water tight enough to get a prosecution and get him locked away.

I made my point clear to both agencies eventually and it was documented in notes by Children's Services. I cannot explain to you the power that this agency has over families. They have an important job to do, and have only one remit, that being to safeguard children from harm, no matter what. However, as part of a pawn in their safeguarding, I was powerless and petrified of them.

I was upfront about my feelings with Julie and Natalie, who both took my scepticism and terror with a pinch of salt, reassuring me that in their eyes, from what they could see at this point I had tried to safeguard my children by moving, and had reported events as soon as they had come to light. I knew though, that we were not out of the woods yet!

They eventually left and we moved on with the next few days in a daze. Bong seemed to have bounced back, being agreeable to a few sessions of counselling with a child counsellor, which was arranged for the following week, at the suggestion of Natalie. I nodded, like the proverbial nodding dog at her suggestions, anything to get them to close our case sooner. The normally feisty and proactive Dan had become a pleaser and was playing the game of her life!

Chapter 43 Scapegoat

On the Saturday of that week it was my brother's, little boy's first birthday celebration in their home town to which we had been invited.

I had not received a reply from my text earlier in the week, so began to type a longer, apologetic message to my brother, explaining our absence from the festivities, later that week.

I hope you're all ok. I know it's the birthday party this week, but I can't come. I am guessing dad will be there. After what I had to tell you this week and everything that has happened I can't be in the same building as him 'I wanted him dead, as in not breathing'!!

I have always been one to wear my heart on my sleeves and honestly thought that my brother would have taken on board what I had told him, and sought to safeguard his son. I thought that he would share my anger and perhaps also wish the bastard dead, as in not breathing too!! I got no reply from the text bizarrely, but concluded that he was just busy with birthday preparations. How wrong I was and how those words, written in a fit of pique would come back to haunt me just a few short weeks later.

After that, everything went quiet. Children's Services kept us on their books, but we had no contact, the children settled down and my head began to clear slightly.

I was still feeling bruised and dented after the issues with my mother two months previously, and couldn't believe that something so drastic had happened so soon after. I began to work on my mindset more and practiced gratitude's and positivity every moment of the day. As my eyes opened I began to think about all the marvellous things I had in my world to be grateful for, and found myself looking for beauty in everything. I immersed myself in learning more about the Law of Attraction and covered my house in positive quotes.

For those of you going through tough times I implore you to find some strength and time to look at the beauty in your life, all around you. Whether that's the blue sky, the birds, the flowers around you, the green of the trees, the frost on the car window, the comfort of your bed or the cup of tea that warms your hands. There is beauty everywhere, and I assure you that finding positives everywhere, and seeking to bring gratitude to your life will enhance your existence much more than you could imagine.

One study that I read found that people who had experienced hardship, adversity and misfortune ended up happier and more content than others with no history of misfortune. I could relate to this so well. I was grateful for my life, my friends, my health and those positive relationships that I had and held them dear. I had always seen the tough times as character building and as a test to make me stronger. My negative experiences had in effect shaped me into the resilient and capable woman I was today. Adversity, not comfort had created change!

Please, please don't see your tough situation as being the end of your life and shaping your whole future. You can move things forward, time passes you can, become stronger, invincible even.

Three weeks after the party I still was in possession of the birthday boys present. I had had no contact from any member of my family and so I decided to hand deliver to my brother's house as I passed that way on business. I had no idea what sort of reception I might receive and had planned to leave the present on the doorstep, in true, cowardly 'Knock Knock Ginger' style and run away.

With my heart pounding with anticipation I drove through their village. I had a horrible intuition that my father might be at the house, but rather than listen to that small voice telling me to turn the car around and head home I continued onto the shared carpark by my brother's house. I scanned the carpark for my father's vibrant, blue car and was relieved when I couldn't see it. Cursing my intuition I climbed out of the car and present in hand walked towards the empty front garden.

As I got a few steps nearer I looked at a hidden car park space that had eluded me as I had driven in. There, parked up was my father's car. I was past the point of no return, committed to the present drop when out of the front door came my brother, carrying his son and my fucking worm of a father. Bewilderment and disbelief overcame me.

My brother had chosen to ignore what I had told him and was still having contact with that monster. What was wrong with these people, I thought irrationally. Refusing to be frightened off I quickened my pace and launched the present over the front gate.

I must have looked like a woman possessed as I approached, as my brother and father stopped in their tracks and stared at me, unable to believe that I had come to the house. Present delivered, or thrown, I turned on my heel and crossed quickly back to the safety of my little red Citroen car. Neither of them moved from their spots, boring holes in the back of my skull until I was driving away.

It was then that the shock hit me. Grief for the relationship with my brother that had been defiled by my father's perversions and for the choices that my brother had made. Once again a family member had voted against me, leaving me feeling so alone and sad. In losing my brother I knew that I had fore-fitted any relationship with my sister or younger brother ever again.

Out of six siblings I was the persona non grata to them all and had no relationship with either parent. I was devastated once again. My positive head told me that it was no great loss while my heart wept at the loneliness and lack of belonging. These wounds would take a while to heal I figured.

Chapter 44 Karma

It was at 8am on a sunny Sunday morning, six weeks later when the phone rang unexpectedly, answering my prayers and changing our lives forever.

I jumped out of bed, unsteady on my feet from my deep slumber, already trying to rationalise who it might be. We tended to not get sales calls on a Sunday, but I guessed there was a first for everything. A little hostile I picked up, 'Hello'

'Dani,' said the familiar voice at the end of the line. It was my great Aunt, who once upon a time I had been close to. Thanks to my father's dealings this relationship had become toxic too.

My heart stopped dead and adrenaline flooded to my knees. 'Is it Grandad, what's happened?' I whispered, fearing the worse.

'It's your dad' she continued, 'He fell in his fishpond last night and drowned'.

'What, dead?' I stupidly asked, like there could be another type of dead, other than the 'not breathing' type!!!

'Yes' she lamented.

'Ah ok, thank you for phoning' I ended the call and turned to Charlie, who by now had sat up in bed, fascinated by the one side of the conversation that he had been witness too. Clearly the word 'dead' had sparked his attention!

'My dad's dead' I said, unable to keep a completely spontaneous smirk from my lips. 'I wished him dead only six weeks ago, I asked karma to deal with him, and she did', I spoke my incredulous thoughts out loud and felt nothing but relief. No remorse, no sadness, no grief, only lightness and joy.

I am sorry, not sorry, if this offends you reader. I have lost those who I loved and have grieved long and hard. The deaths of both of my beautiful nan's broke my soul in two. The death of my father made me smile. He hurt and abused so many people in his lifetime that death, by drowning, whilst pissed was an apt way to end his life. I had begged Charlie for the keys to run him over, but karma has intervened and saved me from a lengthy jail sentence. In the word's of Alanis Morissette, 'isn't it ironic, don't ya think!'

It transpired, via a friend of our family that the turn of events went something like this, however, having never spoken to my siblings or stepmother about that night directly, and having been barred by the family from speaking with the coroner, I cannot say first hand that this is what happened.

It is alleged that my stepmother and younger brother had been at my sister's house and returned to the house after midnight. No-one noticed in the tiny, two up, two down terraced house that the back door was open and that my father was not in his bed. An hour later they found him floating, face down in the pond, swimming with the fishes.

The police were called and he was pronounced dead at the scene. Way to go karma, you're the best!

I wondered if how I was feeling was right, and if at some point shock and tears may get the better of me! To this day I have shed no tears or remorse for his passing. He brought nothing but misery to those whose lives he had touched and I remain glad.

I spent the day with my grandfather, glad that my nan hadn't been alive to see this family tragedy unfold. She had loved my father, he had been her favourite and couldn't bear a bad word said about him. She was in a perpetual state of denial about his alcoholism and was forever granting his pleas of needing money for various things, which in turn enabled him to finance his habit.

My grandfather was stoic as ever, quick to share his counsel with whoever would listen. I am not convinced that my grandfather, being emotionally damaged from his abhorrent childhood during the war had much propensity to love anyone or anything.

'I always knew that bloody alcohol would kill him in the end' he volunteered candidly.

I don't think I ever saw him shed a tear for his deceased son. Sins of the father's and all that!

Having had no contact from my brother for six weeks I figured that now was as good a time as any to check up on him and see if he was holding up ok. I had had a bit of time to come to terms about my brother's choice between me and my dad and I truly bore no malice for his choice.

Putting out the olive branch to him, I began to write

Hi, It's me. I hope you are ok.

I couldn't think of what else to write and kept it short and to the point. I merely wanted to let him know that I was here for him. Once again, nothing was going to prepare me for what happened two days later on a sunny summer's afternoon.

Chapter 45 Harassment

I was cleaning the house, always a fruitless task given that I have six children and enjoying the peace and quiet, whilst looking up to the hills which framed my house. There was a buzzard pair, circling high above, gliding on a thermal and I watched in wonder as they effortlessly wound higher, calling to each other in the cloudless sky. I spent much time in awe at where we had ended up living, both of us dragged up on council estates and now though hard work we lived in this idyll on the side of the beautiful hills. Grateful didn't quite cut it.

Out of my front window as I cleaned the dog slobber and finger prints from the glass, I saw a police car drive slowly by down the cul-de-sac, and this time trusting my intuition I knew that they were calling at my house. Shutting the dog in the kitchen, I waited on my drive for the car to turn around in the street, park up and for a young constable to get out. He was a little taken aback to see me waiting for him on the drive and asked me who I was. I think my coming out to meet him had him immediately on the back foot.

With my name confirmed as being the person he had come to see he introduced himself officiously and asked if he might come in for a chat. I would say at a rough guess he was mid twenties, and loved his job. I cordially invited him in and once seated in the sunlight flooded lounge he began to tell me that my brother had put a complaint into the police for harassment and that he had come round to the house to issue me with a harassment warning.

Well, you couldn't freaking write this shit. Could my family stoop any lower?

Trying desperately to remain calm and not verbally batter the poor man, who was to be fair, just doing his job I asked him on what grounds it felt that I had harassed my brother.

I wanted to hear exactly what pile of crap my brother had told the police in order for them to warrant a visit. He mentioned the three texts which I had sent over the preceding two month's and informed me, that my brother had told them, to tell me that he and the rest of my family wanted no contact with me again. I was informed that I wasn't welcome at the funeral of my father and that if I contacted my brother one more time I would be arrested and charged with harassment. I must have resembled a gold fish, mouth open, gawping at the relayer of stupid notices.

He fished into his pocket and pulled out a small pocket note book and a printed piece of paper. He handed me the printed piece of paper on which it read in bold black type, 'Harassment Notice'. Indicating towards the end of the form he gesticulated that I should now sign the said 'Harassment Notice' which he had diligently produced.

You could have heard a pin drop as I looked at the Notice. What this young officer did not know was that in my day job

I dealt with such notices regularly and knew that I could not be made to sign it. For me, signing it was tantamount to an admission of guilt, and I was not going to admit that I was guilty, just to satisfy my cunt of a brother. (I rarely use such profanities, but in this situation I feel that it is completely warranted!)

'You need to sign here' he instructed helpfully.

'I'm not signing that piece of shit' I ranted, rising from the sofa and standing tall. I quivered with anger and felt like I may just explode.

 'You can tell my cunt of a brother that I never want to see or speak with him ever again. If I want to go to the fucking funeral then I will, it's a fucking public ceremony,' I yelled, having totally lost control, once and for all.

'And, you can tell my fucked up, dumb twats of a family that I might well come with a fucking marching band and drums and dance on his grave, whilst wearing bright yellow' I lambasted, turning to the young officer, who by now was edging towards the lounge door with his mouth aghast.

'Would you consider signing my pocket note book?' He muttered as he slid into the hallway.

I nearly snatched the small book out of his hands and launched it out the door with him, so was my rage.

'Get out NOW' I yelled, 'I have nothing more to say to you'. I opened the front door and watched him leave, unsigned form in hand and walk dejectedly to his car. I could hear him mentally thinking 'That didn't go as planned'!!!

Too fecking right it didn't, I mused as I slid down the back of the front door, wondering just what I must had done in a past life to deserve such knobs for family.

I sat, for a while in my hall, slow box breathing and concentrating on the azure blue sky and the beautiful hills outside my window. I focused upon the beauty and strength of the hills and all the positive things in my life while trying not to let tear's get the better of me.

I felt that if I started crying I would never let up. After what seemed like hours had passed I chanced a look at my watch. It was pick up time and I knew that I needed to regain my calm façade before I collected my children from school. I absolutely didn't want them to be witness to yet more stress and upset.

I knew that my family would be hoping for a reaction from me about their abhorrent actions. I could picture them sitting wondering if I had been ' told off' by the police, rubbing their dirty hands in delight as they thought that they had the upper hand. I knew that they would take the time to stalk my social media profile, so decided to rile them slightly.

Pre my positive days I would have whinged and whined about the injustice of the whole scenario, crying and bleating to anyone who would lend an ear. However, invincibility cloak buttoned up and Batfink wings wrapped around me, I refused to roll over and be affected by their negativity.

Standing in front of my huge, floor to ceiling window, with views over the valley I took an exquisite photograph of the blue sky, the lush, green vegetation and the soaring buzzards, gliding on the thermals and reviewed my handiwork. It was a picture-book photograph which could have been a poster. Sniggering, I uploaded it to my Facebook account with the words

What a simply stunning day. #Blessed #Gratitude #Beauty

If they thought that they could break me, they were going to be surprised at my strength and seeming ignorance of their activities. I giggled to myself at the concern that they would all share around the funeral and they worry that I might just rock up with a marching band to celebrate his death. I imagined them trying to keep the funeral details a secret until the eleventh hour.

Chapter 46 The Black Sheep

In full super-sleuth mode, over the forth coming week I made a number of calls to try and find out where the funeral may be, and where my father was being held prior to the funeral. I was in luck when I came across a slip of paper whilst at my grandfather's house on his table, upon which had been written the name of the undertakers and the date of the funeral. I am not sure if it had been left there deliberately, but it saved me playing Miss Marple any more.

Over the next few days I mentioned to my grandfather's cleaner, who happened to be good friends with some of the haters about the date of the funeral, how I was planning to take a day off from work to go along. To add credence to my plans I dropped in that I knew the venue was in the local village church and which undertakers the family had instructed for the whole sorry event.

I wanted the family to know that I knew, and to be on tenterhooks for the whole event. Whilst I had no intention of going, for I had nothing to grieve for, I wanted to play the role of the bitch that they had convinced themselves that I was. I don't feel that I was being petty. I am a dreadful tease and saw it as one large practical joke at their expense. Call to a penance to them for their treatment of me.

I did however have one actual plan to carry out in order to put my mind at ease once and for all. You may think this weird, but I wanted to go and see my father's body in the Chapel of Rest. I needed to know that he was dead for myself and that he was gone forever. My mind kept imagining that it was all one big joke and he was not actually dead. Irrational, I know but my thoughts, all the same.

I could not have imagined the rigmarole that I would occur when I called the undertakers to relay my request a few days before the funeral. I would not have thought that my stepmother would have briefed them about the 'black sheep, bitch of a daughter' of the deceased, yet she had!.

So, whilst the undertaker was very apologetic that she was unable to allow me to visit, I took the time to tell her a bit about the deceased and his proclivity for abusing children. I explained that I did not need to see his face, just his coffin, in order to begin to heal. I hated the unfairness that allowed her to share with someone who did not know me her thoughts about me, and so decided to have my right to reply in a frank and uncensored fashion.

After a pregnant pause, she said that she was going to call my stepmother and try and get her to agree to my very reasonable request. She was merely doing her job and abiding by her client's wishes. I cordially thanked her and awaited her call back. Within thirty minutes the call came to confirm that I was allowed to the funeral parlour around fifty minutes away, from my home the following day. It amused me greatly that my family had sought to instruct the services an undertaker such a way out of their local town, in order to throw me off the scent! Was there no end to their vindictiveness and stupidity?

Overnight, I was restless, my dreams plagued with coffins that opened, bodies bloated from water immersion and my stepmother and siblings ranting at others, telling them what a disgusting human being I was. It was fitful sleep that left me feeling drained and exhausted when I finally got up to get the children ready for school.

I felt sick and was tempted to admit that I had bitten off more than I could chew this time! I tried to thrash out in my head why I needed to go to see the coffin and work out the pros and cons for both courses of action. No matter how I looked at the scenario and how petrified I was, I knew that for my own sanity, I needed to go and set eyes on the coffin that day.

With trepidation, I dropped the children off to school and set off on the drive. It was raining hard, with grey clouds billowing fast across the sky which distracted me as I drove. They were an exact reflection of the turbulence going on in my mind, with my black thoughts racing at hundreds of miles per hour.

I still wasn't sure that I was doing the right thing, but pressed on. I felt unable to ask a friend or my husband to come with me, seeing it as a sign of weakness. I have never been good at asking for help or support, choosing to, more often than not, just crack alone. I hate showing vulnerabilities.

The drive was long, but after just under an hour I reached a small undertakers on the corner of an obscure residential road. The family had clearly chosen this for a reason!

With my heart beating out of my chest I pulled up opposite the Funeral Directors premises and got out of the car. My legs flooded with adrenaline felt shaky and I once again longed for the hand of my strong and capable husband, just for a moment. It was like being caught in a dreadful nightmare, when your legs won't work and you seem to be walking through treacle.

Eventually I crossed the road and entered what looked like someone's living room! Inside the reception was a kind looking woman who instantly seemed to know who I was, as she ushered me without uttering a word towards the Chapel of Rest.

Down a tiny corridor we came to a comically small room, carpeted in red, with a couple of candles burning. To my right, by the white wall was the white coffin which contained my father.

Tears rolled down my face as I stood stock still, unable to move towards the final resting place of the man who had tried his damnedest to ruin me, to slander my name and reputation to anyone who would listen, who had tried to abuse my son, who had defiled both me and my aunt and had abused my mother. That monster, lying in a cheap wooden box was finally gone and could harm no one else. I didn't shed those tears for him, I shed them for what should have been and what I had lost. For the kind and caring fathers that I saw and never had, for the distress and shock I should never have had to contend with, and for all the other wrongs which had contributed to the life I had lived at his hands. So many regrets and so much to hate him for, yet I struggled to feel hate, just sadness.

For what seemed like a lifetime I stood still, unable to move, locked in position in front of the casket. Suddenly, as if possessed by an invisible and invincible force I was able to move, as if finding a magnificent strength in his death and absolute lack of power over me after forty years had made me stronger than ever.

I walked up to the coffin.

'I'm glad you're dead' I told him, 'Good riddance.'

And, with that I turned on my heel and walked straight out of the building, immensely glad that I had gone to bid him farewell. My fortitude and resilience at that moment was greater than ever and I was grateful for the life that had gone before me, giving me the chance to be all I could be, more than either of my parents ever thought possible and developing me into a resourceful and strong woman who seemed to sport an invincibility cloak.

Chapter 47 R&R

That week went by smoothly, with a call from Natalie, the social worker telling me that she was going to close the case, given that my father was now dead.

I cried brazenly in the street at that moment and saw it as a demarcation of what had gone before. The bad times moving on through to the good days, which I knew were ahead of us.

With the summer holidays stretching out in front of us, we packed up our car and crammed all six children into the Mazda Bongo to travel an epic eight hundred miles to the Ardeche in France for a much-needed holiday.

I felt lighter, calmer and immensely grateful that I had come though some of the most traumatic times ever, slightly greyer, but intact, with my beautiful and thoughtful children and rock of a husband beside me. The kids were growing fast and whilst cramped in the car for nearly twenty four hours we laughed, sang, ate and chatted on our long drive.

Our three weeks were spent swimming, walking, sun bathing and reading. The evenings were packed with family time, with good food, wine and games. I have never been so grateful for the sun, mountains and a suntan.

I grew mentally stronger and was looking forward to returning home relaxed and chilled. I was unable to predict the events that would shock and surprise me, just a few days after our return.

Chapter 48 No, You Couldn't make This Up!

It was a beautiful, sunny afternoon. The sky was a brilliant, flawless blue. The buzzards and hand gliders lazily drifted in the warm thermals above me and I lay reading on the wooden steamer lounger on my decking, soaking up the sun and losing myself in the plot.

My mobile phone rang, a gentle trill, but an annoyance nether the less with a private number. Ever skeptical I answered, expectantly, on the defensive, ready to be told that I could claim money for a non-existent accident for the fiftieth time that month.

A stern voice connected, 'Is that Danielle Downey?' the nameless voice intruded.

'To whom am I speaking?' I countered with equal formality.

'It's DI Carter, CID, from Union Street Police Station, I was wondering if you might be available to come down this afternoon for a chat with me?' he asked.

I felt my heart stop and my knees buckle. What the fucking hell did they want now? The bastard was dead and buried and yet, still managed to plague me from his watery grave. Trying to remain calm and lucid I asked, 'What is it about?'

I couldn't bring myself to utter any more words in my sentence for fear that my voice might crack,

'We'd rather chat to you in person, than over the phone. We've got some questions about a text that you wrote to your brother some weeks before your father drowned' his calm voice explained.

In an instant, I put two and two together, and fought to maintain a controlled voice as I deduced exactly what he wanted to chat to me about and just who had instigated his call and the involvement of CID.

'If you want to speak with me, on a Sunday afternoon, you can come to my house. I am not setting foot inside a police station, and before you come you had better give me a heads up about what you want to speak about, otherwise you are not welcome' I maintained.

With a sigh, he appeared to register what I had said and before hanging up the phone he said, 'I'll see you in thirty minutes'.

The phone clicked off and I once again wondered just when this nightmare was going to end. Unable to think straight or rationally, I ran upstairs to find my Spock like husband , whom I knew had my back and my brain in moments like this. Explaining to him the brief contents of the call I tried to focus on what I could do to help myself before PC Plod arrived. I am aware, reader that this makes me sound like I am guilty as a puppy in the poo.

I have told you before that I wanted to kill the bastard, dead, as in with not breathing, but just couldn't find the opportunity to do it.

However, it appeared to me that someone in my family wanted to implicate me in his death. I wouldn't have minded, if I could have said honestly that I did kill him! How fucking ironic was this?

Mr Rational decided that we needed some guidance from a friend of ours who was a police sergeant. I by this time was becoming increasingly more hysterical and panicky, which was ludicrous, given my innocence, yet this didn't stop my knees knocking and hands shaking.

I just about dialled her number and she answered hesitantly, given that I never, ever called her. She was one of the few however, to know the explicit, sordid details of theist few months. Simpering like the village idiot I tried to explain what had happened.

Taking the phone from my sweaty grasp Charlie filled our friend in about the turn of events and listened to her response. I had begun to think that I was going to be arrested and carted off to the nick, for a crime that I didn't commit, but bloody well wanted to.

She advised, that if I was being formally suspected as a suspect to murder, then I would be arrested, and interviewed, under caution. There would be no pussy-footing around visiting me at home, over a cuppa!

She advised me to ask in what capacity they wanted to chat, before I said anything and what made them approach me, two months after his death. Don't, whatever you do tell them that you wanted him dead! As Charlie relayed this to me the front door knocked, the dog went crazy and I tried to keep my heart from beating out of my chest and mind from shattering.

Why, you might ask, was I so bothered by the police's presence in the house? I can only put it down to early childhood memories of my father being pulled over in the car, around once a week, by the local traffic cops for traffic violations or car issues. I recall, being small and terrified, as this leathered up, giant of a police man would wave the car to a stop and approach the wound down window. I was terrified that as my father was asked to get out of the car that I could be left alone and he would be thrown into prison.

To this day, I still openly recoil if a police car drives past me, even if it is going in the opposite direction. Does anyone else feel guilty at the very presence of the police, or is it just me? Heaven forbid, I was pulled over by a traffic cop, I cry like a baby!

Anyway, back to that dreadful Sunday, which wasn't actually that dreadful, but felt like one of the most challenging days of my life. It's strange how with the balance of hindsight things are not as bad as we felt them to be at the time! Time, for me has proved to be a true healer, as is that positive and resilient mindset.

So, the dog went crazy and I hid downstairs on my decking, not wanting the negativity energy associated with my asshole brother and his text allegations to infect my happy and vibrant home. Charlie opened the door to the voice on the end of the phone and showed him downstairs.

'My wife would rather we speak outside, because of the kids' he explained as he led the CID officer downstairs to the decking.

I paced the decking like a caged animal, holding in the urge to scream at the injustice of this, yet as the policeman stepped outside I sat my butt on a seat and did not say a word, waiting for him to explain his presence. It was unusual for me to be silent. Charlie sensed this and tried to speak first.

'I'm sorry to disturb your Sunday afternoon, Danielle, but we have some questions that we think you might be able to answer, regarding the death of your father and some texts which you sent to your brother six weeks before his death.' He asked seriously.

'Would you like to tell me what you know about this please?' He continued.

He handed me a sheet of white A4 paper on which in extra-large font was printed a section of the text which I had sent to my brother in the week after Bong's disclosure. It read

You know that I want him dead, as in not breathing. I hate him for all that he has done.

The malice of what my brother and my siblings had done hit me and my hands shook hard as I read and reread the extract.

'Did you send that?' the officer asked, knowing full well that I did, as my phone number had been screen shotted onto the paper along with those hateful words.

Gone was the calm exterior, the Stone face of which Genghis Khan spoke, when dealing with the enemy, giving nothing away. Replacing it was a shocked and angry woman, who couldn't believe the manipulation involved in this latest debacle.

Unable to control the words which flew from my mouth like a volcano I answered him with venom.

'Yes, I did. I meant every fucking word and wish I had killed him. I wish that it had been my size five foot print that you had found imprinted on the back of his head' I admitted with gusto.

Tears rolled down my face in a torrent and I continued, while Charlie stood behind the officer, gesticulating frantically, to tell me to shut up.

'Had you not noticed that my brother only copied two lines from what was a loving and compassionate text that I sent to him? I thought you were Investigating officers! Did you not ask him to see the rest of the text?' I asked incredulously.

'No, we didn't see the rest. He bought this copy into Castle Street, yesterday and thought we might be interested in it.

'He's trying to imply that I murdered him' I mouthed to myself, wrenching my hands and tapping my feet to abate the anger and confusion that ran wild in my head.

'We know that you were no-where near the house on the night he died, we've done our checks' he reassured.

'You actually checked the traffic cameras for our cars' I laughed ironically. 'trust me, if I was going to kill him I would have walked and swam through the river, and then I would have confessed my crime, with pride.'

'The Coroner wanted to know why you would send a text like this, wishing him dead, and how come, six weeks later he is found face down in a pond,' he asked.

I felt like I was in a Monty Python sketch. We were going from the sublime to the freaking ridiculous.

'Have you read the child protection notes about my son's disclosure, about what he did to me, to my mum, to his sister? I wrote that text to my brother, after YOU, the police told me I should make my brother aware of his proclivity for all children, and not just girls as I thought. It's nothing to do with me that karma took control and dealt with him for me' I divulged, more calmly now.

'Karma?' he looked confused.

'Karma, you know, what goes around, comes around, and all that jazz; The Law of Reciprocity and such like.' I tried to explain, knowing that he wouldn't get it!

'Not sure I believe in that mumbo jumbo, but I guess it answered your call that day! As a parent, I can relate to your feelings for him, totally. We all want to protect our kids and woe betide anyone who crosses me,' he said with genuine concern and empathy to our situation.

I saw him as more human now, and less CID officer. He seemed like a kind man, who felt sorry that this pile of crap had landed at my door.

I had given him the answer that he needed to satiate the Coroner and that was his job done.

'I am genuinely sorry that I had to come and drag all this up again for you,' he said as he touched my arm. 'Look after her Charlie' he said, loud enough for me to hear.

He made for the door back through the house and was shown out, into the bright, afternoon sunshine, while I took a few moments to compose myself. I felt battle worn and exhausted. When would this end?

Chapter 49 Resilience

What drives someone to be so vindictive and callous, was and still is totally beyond me. Whether it was grief or a need to try and punish me for daring to rock the boat I don't know.

Maybe in my disclosure and that of others dragged up personal issues relating to their childhood experiences. I guess I'll never know, and have no desire to understand.

That afternoon, I sat back on my lounger and looked at the world in which I lived. Despite the darker times, I felt grateful that I could appreciate the beauty around me and still had a warm, empathetic and compassionate heart, despite the challenges which had arisen since my birth.

I knew that out of these challenges would grow yet more strength and resilience and that I could learn so much from these harsh lessons to help me grow.

As I posted a picture of a fish pond that afternoon on Social Media I felt strong and invincible. If my family were watching for signs of me self-destructing, I was not going to show them this outwardly.

I had told only a few close friends about the past few months and their revelations, and they got the significance of the pond. Others, merely thought that I was building a new fish pond! My family, well, I guess they might have been shocked at my audacity, but did I care? Not a freaking jot!

Chapter 50 Broken

Life went on and the trauma of the last few months began to take its toll. I had days when I could barely function and other days when I was absolutely on fire. The temptation to go to the GP to get some mind-numbing drugs to help me to stop the negative thoughts and destructive self-chat was huge, but I resisted.

I am not saying that I am against prescription drugs to help you to cope. I had taken Citralipam for six months when I first had the flash backs and went for sexual abuse counselling. They helped me to feel numb, and not care. I felt emotionally dead and stared into space for eons, not thinking, just being. For a while, this suited me.

Charlie remarked how much I sat down, just looking at stuff, with a glazed look in my eyes, and how in ten years he had never seen me so still. But I knew that this type of apathetic zombie facade wasn't right for me in the long run. I needed to feel, feel the good, the bad and the downright ugly with all of my emotions, otherwise I may as well be dead!

As I weened myself off of these small white tablets I had began to feel more like me. I felt joy and hate, felt love and anger and felt pride and passion. Six months as a virtual zombie had given me a rest, but I was back to being me, and I felt good.

I had fought an internal battle for a long while over the use of anti-depressants. I saw them as the weak option and couldn't work out why so many people took them and relied on them. I think my attitude was down to complete ignorance and the fear of failing and letting myself down. I didn't think that people who used anti-depressants were weak, I just didn't think that I was in need of them.

In reality, I cried a lot of the time, over reacted at the slightest thing and couldn't get my thoughts into a rational order. The smallest task felt huge and couldn't work out what to do first when doing a simple thing like making a cup of tea. For the first time in my life I felt weak and vulnerable. For someone who had never felt able to rely completely on anyone, bar myself this was a scary place to find myself in. Unable to rely upon me, because I was slowly falling apart and unable to show my vulnerabilities to anyone close to me, left me isolated and desperate.

The turning point came for me when I was studying in Bristol on a course every month for three days at a time. It was during a lecture from a mental health doctor who spent two hours taking the group through the role of drugs with victims of domestic abuse.

I listened as she explained that when the body is exposed to stress over a protracted period of time, it becomes unable to react to the stress and stops producing the anti-stress hormones. A bit like trying to flush a toilet which has no more water in it, the body when it has no stress relieving hormone left, stops producing it completely. This means that the tank is empty, leaving the body to deal with the stressors alone. The talk was like a light bulb flicking on, finally. I had been exposed to so much stress and struggle that my tank, my innate coping mechanisms were on strike!

Finally, after thirty-nine years, they had become redundant! The lecturer explained that certain anti-depressants worked with the body to switch on the receptors again and get the cycle back up and running. Having a small amount of the anti-stress hormone resulted in the body being able to produce more. Bingo, this was just what I needed to hear. I wasn't a failure, I wasn't broken, I was me. A lifetime of shite had resulted in me transitioning from 'functioning mad', to broken.

Ever the control freak, and given a choice to make the situation better I knew immediately that I needed a trip to the GP on my return. I was mildly thrilled to be presented with a solution and felt grateful for the information. With trepidation, on my walk back to the station I called the GP and asked to urgently see a doctor the following day. I didn't tell my husband that evening what I had planned.

There is still so much stigma around anti-depressants and I couldn't bear for him to look at me and see a weak and broken woman. I needed to tell him the back story and just why I was going to take the drugs and what I hoped to achieve from their use. He needed to be able to rationalise the drug and see it as a positive.

Having taken the six children to school that morning I headed off to the doctors for my early morning appointment. My heart pounded as I sat patiently in the crowded waiting room, and I nearly walked out every minute or so. Thankfully, the session was not running too far behind and within fifteen minutes I was sitting in-front of my very lovely, female doctor.

'What can I do for you today?' she asked, swivelling her chair to face me.

Through snot and snivelling I told her how I wasn't mad, just stressed, how I was working through sexual abuse counselling, dealing with family issues, parenting six children, virtually on my own, while my husband worked away and how some days I found it hard to cope.

Telling another health professional took great guts on my behalf. I was terrified that she might label me as absolutely crackers, call in the psych. team and cart me off to some institution to partake in country dancing, basket weaving and painting by numbers for the rest of my days. How freaking irrational was I and how little did I love myself back then!

I can see now, that I needed time to heal and mend, and that I was worth that investment. I know that I am over critical of myself and my perceived failures and was even more so back then. The ability to love myself, warts and all, has taken many years for me. I urge you, to be kind to yourself, listen to your body and love you. Because, without the love of you, how can you expect others to love and cherish you too?

The GP listened and without prompting validated what I had told her, with a simple 'You've been through such a lot, you are very strong and inspiring.'

Part of that self-love is an allowance to accept compliments easily. Being told that I was strong and inspiring just upset me more back then. It was a recognition of my life and its struggles, and the fact that someone else believed me and what I had been through meant so much.

I told the GP about the analogy of the toilet cistern and how I believed Citralipam worked and why I believed that I needed it. I felt, with absolute clarity that this was the right course of action. The GP needed no convincing and was writing a prescription as I spoke.

'I want the lowest dose possible though' I said, refusing to give up all control! I bet she thought I was a complete pain in the arse, but she didn't let on as she patiently made me another appointment to come back two weeks later for a review.

'It can take around two weeks for these to get into your system, and you can get some nasty side effects' she warned.

I bounced out of the office, not caring if I grew black nipple hairs, or warts on my nose as a side effect, if it meant that I felt more like me again! I went home and marked six months ahead in my diary, which was around February time. I was going to allow myself six months only on these drugs, so they had better bloody well work. I was not going to allow myself to be a slave to the medication. I took the tablet that afternoon and waited for the change.

Disappointedly, I couldn't feel the effects until three days in, when unable to stand the smell or thought of food and unable to rouse myself out of my chair, I finally felt my body responding to the drug.

I sat and looked out of the window for two hours, limbs heavy and mind quieter than it had been for ages. I felt silenced, like the world could implode around me and I would look around and not react. It was like being in the body of a completely apathetic person. These effects grew stronger, as did the nausea. I dreamt bright, vivid and violent dreams whilst on the drugs and woke up every morning feeling as if I had battled through the night, single handedly taking on the woes of the world.

Ever positive, with the 'every cloud has a silvery lining' kind of attitude I lost weight and felt slimmer than I had done for a long-time. I didn't account for the loss of my libido and for the first time in years had no interest in my husband. I performed out of wifely duty for the first time ever and whilst I craved his touch and hugs, couldn't have given two hoots about the sex.

He got used to me sitting down, watching the world going by, without the concentration to read a book, cognitive ability switched off, in a kind of trance like state.

'I've never known you be so still' he commented one Sunday afternoon as I watched him build decking. Normally, I would be up there working hard with him. I couldn't summon up the energy or enthusiasm to help at all. I stopped raising my voice and couldn't get excited about anything.

With six children in the house, all under fourteen I had been prone to having to raise my voice as a last resort to get stuff done. I found on the Citralipram that I just couldn't get angry! The kids were delighted, they had some sort of drone for a mother who agreed to everything, for a quiet life and was a shadow of her former self! I was a Step-ford Wife, but without the desire to have sex or cook!

Chapter 51 Mended

My mother and sister thought that it was marvellous that I was on the drugs. They had labelled me as 'prickly and difficult to get on with 'yet, with my current inability to challenge anything or fight back, I was the model daughter and sister.

What I began to notice after four months on the drug was that my thoughts cleared and I began to hanker after the Danielle of old. The ballsy, passionate and feisty woman who would stand up to bullies and try to make wrongs right. I spoke with Charlie about coming off the drugs, yet the thought seemed to terrify him. 'what if you get worse' he asked with trepidation.

I tried to reassure him that I was feeling better and that I didn't want to be a slave to the drugs for ever, and that I had planned to start withdrawing from the drugs within the next few days. I did not want to just stop taking them, and risk going 'cold turkey', so, in atypical style for me I read on forums and googled the life out of ' withdrawing from Citralipram'.

I came to the conclusion that I could reduce my dose minutely, week by week over six weeks and be off the drugs by the following February.

Blade in hand, on my chosen Sunday morning I began to cut up my tablets and take control. I looked like a hardened addict, cutting off fine slices from my tiny tablets and dabbing the dust with my finger, before popping it into my mouth to lick off the fine particles, making sure that I didn't reduce too quickly.

Six weeks later I was free of those tiny white pills. I didn't tell anyone that I was off them, I held that secret close to my heart. The first time that I raised my voice to reprimand one of the children, Charlie immediately asked if I should go back onto the tablets.

My reaction was venomous. He had got so used to this quiet and placid wife that he thought that my normal behaviour was abnormal! It took a few weeks for him to fall back into sync with the wife that he had loved, who looked after six children and was prone to an outburst or two. I wasn't going mad, I didn't need medicating, I was just me!

I am a great believer that there is a time and a place for anti-depressant drugs and that if you need them, it's ok. There is still too much stigma attached within our society regarding mental illness, stress and medication. Yet without these drugs, I don't think that I would be here today. The comment by the lecturer, on the day I decided to see my GP has stuck in my head ever since, she said

'Thirty percent of the population take anti-depressants, and the other seventy percent who are not taking them, probably should be!'.

Don't be shy, don't be stubborn and don't wait. You'll be amazed at the number of people who confide in you that they too have resorted to medication at one time or another. Life is stressful and challenging from time to time and its always ok to seek help.

I used to believe that showing weakness was a bad thing. Of course now I now that it's a natural reaction to feeling safe and is a normal and natural human reaction. We cannot always be Superwoman or Superman all of the time!

I experienced burnout because of my need to show the world how strong and resilient I was. Had I allowed myself to occasionally admit to myself and others that I was struggling, then I may have allowed myself to seek help far sooner.

Allowing myself to feel vulnerable and show my vulnerability to others is a natural progression in my healing process. Of course I am still a high functioning, tenacious and driven woman, yet I am proud to show my softer side. I can cry with the best of you, weep at movies and be moved to tears by a beautiful sunset. I no longer look upon myself as a failure or weak.

I know now that I could not have come through my childhood and the trauma that I have faced as an adult if I was weak. I am immensely strong and capable. I have learnt to accept that not everyone has my resilience or inner strength, and that by virtue, they are not weak nor failures either. They have just been fortunate enough to not have had the same level of trauma and angst that was bestowed upon me for many years and forced me to develop a higher than normal level of resilience.

So, I am guessing that you may be wanting to know a bit about where my life has got me to now? Have I ended up rocking in a corner, doing basket weaving in the local hospital? Have I finally taken the road to personal destruction and begun taking drugs and drinking to excess? Have I become a wizened up old prune, full of hate that my life and fate dealt poor me so much crap?

The answer to your questions is of course, NO. Why would I want to press that self destruct button after so many years? Why would I want to let myself to become black hearted and bitter? Why would I want to live a sad, dark, unfulfilling life?

The truth is, that I don't want any of those bad things. I never wanted the bad things to happen to me, they just did! I was unlucky, dealt a poor hand with family maybe, but that's it. I have learnt that there is always someone far, far worse off than you, someone who is in danger, sick, distressed, confined, tortured, hurting!

I, in my desperation to survive, have actively created a life filled with beauty, happiness, love, joy, passion, laughter, fulfilment and light. It is no more than I deserve. You see, when you learn to value yourself, to love yourself and respect yourself, you realise that you are entitled to these things.

It was as a result of my journey of self love that I came to realise that my story IS powerful and unique. Maybe to some it's even inspiring? As my confidence and self love grew so did my desire grow to share my journey in a book. The highs and the significant lows. The desperate moments when I thought of suicide, when I could not face another day, and those beautiful moments when I found strength to just keep going. I knew that if I could inspire just one person to keep going, to never give top that I would have fulfilled my ambition.

Chapter 52 Here And Now

After the shock and angst of the difficult times, life has calmed down. The children continue to grow, to eat like locusts and the terrible teenagers have developed into beautiful adult human beings! Remember folks, that your teenager is a beautiful adult just waiting to evolve. There is beauty under the grunting, swearing, moodiness and angst!

As I write this the four older ones are creating their own paths and have flown the nest. My job in being a mother was to give them tools to allow them to grow and develop into kind, thoughtful and confident members of society. They have made it to university, The Army, into nannying jobs and a sports course.

They have made me very proud by virtue of the hardships that they have all endured, and I see that through those hardships they too have developed tenacity and resilience. I see a lot of my natural tenacity and loyalty in the younger two children. They are focused, happy with a strong sense of what is right and wrong. They have an empathy like I have not seen in young children and like me, love to help someone who is in crisis or trouble.

I have a job that I loved and that gave me the ability to help women who needed protection from domestic abuse. It allowed me to advocate, and be a voice for those women who were vulnerable and needed support.

My tenacity and ability to find solutions and never take NO for an answer has enabled me to help others to change their lives and stay safe.

Only four years ago, in the aftermath of the family crap, we became so broke that we needed food parcels. Despite such a challenging time, I am still able to look back and see that in becoming so poor and nearly losing our home some good came out of it.

Having times of financial hardship, both as a child and as an adult has made me appreciate our life now. We are financially stable and secure, with no more money worries. It has allowed me to realise just how precarious life can be when you have a struggle for money, month in, month out.

Having more money now, means that I can help others. I know how tough life can be when you have nothing and am naturally generous of heart. If I can help someone out who is in need to have more then I do it willingly. I know that money brings out the best and worst in people. It can make you miserly or generous. I know which one I'd rather be known as!

If we had not been so broke I would never have looked into network marketing as a way to make some extra cash each month to help me to feed my children. I had used my natural propensity to make a situation better by selling things on eBay and doing car boot sales, yet it was never sustainable. My childhood experiences shaped my refusal to just sit back and accept our worsening situation as one which we were tied to for life.

I look back on being stoney broke with fondness and gratitude. The changes that have occurred within me since starting my home based business are completely incomprehensible. I am more positive, more outgoing, more ballsy and more focused on my goals and what I want my life to look like.

My business has afforded me choices, security and a fabulous extra income which has allowed us to make amazing memories. I have been able to take my time in writing this book as I work my business around my family and my other commitments. Had I not been broke and on the bread line I would never, in all probability, found the time to write because I would have been tied to the hamster wheel of a working day!

If I had not met some amazing people through the self development that is encouraged within the network marketing world, I would never, ever have been brave enough to start putting pen to paper! Seeing other people come through challenges, hardship and face fear, they inspired me to begin my author's journey and write this book.

My relationships with my family remain fragmented and fraught. My mum and I have reconnected after three long years and finally spoken at great length about our relationship. We have seen each other every three-ish and it was easy. We are the mirror image of each other and have so many of the same mannerisms that it is uncanny, given that we have in all probability spent around two whole years in each other's presence.

I have learnt that I don't need her love, her support and her constant reassurance in order to heal. I have accepted the relationship for what it is. The odd text and the occasional day out shopping. I no longer think about when she might call me or text me, and I no longer count the days between phone calls. I have freedom and know that the relationship is more balanced, more equal.

I have never cried a tear of remorse for my father passing away. When I watch my husband playing and interacting with our children it sparks the occasional, fleeting feeling of sadness for what was and what should have been. But, I know that I cannot change what was. It is done.

I have not had contact with any of my six siblings for around four years. Our worlds are totally different, as were our experiences. For them all I guess that it is too difficult a realisation to see exactly what I went through and to accept that our lives were and have been very different. I rejoice when I see my friends experiencing a close relationship with their siblings, but have reached an acceptance that I cannot control others, their reactions or their thoughts. I can only control me!

My friends are my family whom I choose and I am immensely grateful for those who chose to be in my network sharing their love, support and guidance so readily. I try to tell them all how grateful I am to have them in my life and how lucky I am that life brought us to each other.

Without the trials and challenges that life has thrown at me in the years before I found myself and decided to tell my story, I would never have become the person who stands before you today. The strong, resilient, focused, determined, empathetic, loving and warm woman was formed as a result of challenges faced from birth through to forty.

I would not change my past for love nor money.

I don't mean to sound contrite, as I know many people say that they don't believe people when they say such things but, reader without the neglect, emotional horrors, sexual abuse and traumas that I have endured in my life thus far I would not be me!

Chapter 53 My Lessons

From my challenges I learnt many things.

I LEARNT HOPE

That something good always comes along if you believe hard enough. That by refusing to give up and focusing on changing your situation, you can have a positive impact upon it. Whilst I don't agree with animal testing at all, I read a study about resilience which featured poor rats.

The rodents were put into a jar filled with water. They were left to swim round and round in a jar for hours to see if they decided to swim or die. Some who were then rescued and then put back into the same hopelessness of the watery jar, swam for another two hundred and forty hours more than those who had not been rescued. They had hope!

I had hope. I just needed to keep swimming and survive. The beautiful moments in my childhood, the love from my nan, my grandma and my aunt gave me hope.

My love of music, laughter and dancing filled my heart with joy and gave me hope that life could be better. My positive outlook began with hope and a deep knowing that life could get better.

I will never roll over and just give up. I know that there is always more that you can do and more that you can change. Make a choice NOW, that you will never, ever cow down to hopelessness.

I LEARNT RESILIENCE.

I know that having a deep inner strength is more valuable than all the gold in the world, as without it, at the first hurdle we would crumble and die. I developed a resilience as a child that many adults did not have, yet it framed my personality. I am problem focused, self motivated and up for a challenge.

My natural tenacity and spirit in the face of adversity is what got me through the days when I felt alone, unloved and hopeless. I knew that as soon as I was able, I would run way to my aunts and refuse to return home and that would be the day that marked the change in my life. I just had to dig in, despite the torment, the abuse and the horror and make it through each day. Resilience can be learned and honed.

We can all improve our resilience by deciding to change an outlook to problems in our lives. We can chose to acknowledge that tomorrow can be better than today was, and accept that in every problem or challenge there is a lesson.

I LEARNT LOVE

I learnt to love and value those around me, namely my aunt, grand mothers and friends who loved me with all their heart, yet who were unable to change my situation because I told no-one of it.

I learnt to cherish the hugs, the kind words and make them the focus of my tougher days. I knew that I could have developed a black heart, full of self pity and angst. I could have become angry and focused on destroying myself and others in order to prove that I was a bad person and didn't deserve love. Yet, I knew that for me, love could and would change everything.

I love my relationships, my friends, my health and my destiny. I love my future and all that is to come before me, good and bad.

I have learnt to love and appreciate the blue sky, the birds, the sea, the breeze, bright red cherries, the breath in my lungs, the sun on my face and books. My heart is filled with so much to love that this has, more often than not squashed the fires around me into embers, allowing me to walk over those hot coals and escape what many had told me was impossible.

I LEARNT ABOUT DESTINY

As a child we can become predisposed into patterns of behaviour and circumstances that can seek to define our futures in a negative way. If we allow negativity to take hold we will be choked and confined by it.

Negativity can constrain our hopes and our goals, fill our minds with negative chat and make us exude a negative persona that is not who we truly are. I knew that one day, I was going to write a book, that this was written in the stars, and in tablets of stone. Yet, had I listened to my negative inner voice, the one who criticises, chastises and ridicules me I would never have even considered putting my words onto paper.

What I know, having learnt to ignore that inner voice, is that my story, of hardship and transformation may inspire just one person to make a change, to just hang on in there and move their situation forward. If this is the case, my job is done. I have left the world a better place than whence I landed on it forty four years ago!

I knew early on that my destiny was so much more than the suffering, anguish and pain which I was enduring. I want to use my trauma as a force for good and to show you that YOUR destiny is exactly that, IT'S YOURS. You always have a choice and can chose to have a voice.

Your voice, your inner guidance and belief might be just a tiny whisper or an echo today. But tomorrow, next week, next year, whenever, with hope, love, resilience and belief your voice can get louder and louder.

I LEARNT ABOUT SELF MOTIVATION

If I had not done the things that I needed to do, daily tasks, learning, planning and in later years washing my clothes and feeding myself, then no-one would do them for me.

Today I will not hear the word CAN'T. It is not in my vocabulary. As a child laying a carpet with a pair of scissors, tacks and a saucepan was a turning point for my confidence and belief that IF I WANT TO DO ANYTHING, I CAN.

Whether it is starting a new business, running a half marathon, moving a seemingly immovable object or conquering a fear. I can and I WILL. No excuses, no bull shit sob story, JUST FINDING A WAY.

I may have had many set backs along the way, but I know that I will always find a way to do achieve my goals and move forward.

My journey into adulthood, with the hills and mountains that I climbed was made easier by my childhood. The 'just getting through one day at a time' mentality is a mantra that you can use to help you to focus and realise that time passes, second by second, minute by minute, hour by hour. It does not stop for you to examine every aspect of your life that you struggle with.

Know that you have a choice. You can fight the time, live in the past, or you can look forward. By all means acknowledge your pain and suffering, unfairness and hardship, but know that with the going down of the sun at night, and the rising of the sun the following day that the power to change your life is absolutely in your hands.

Stop looking back. See beauty in your life, even if you have to look damn hard to find it. Feel grateful for the breath in your lungs, the sky above you and the firm earth under foot, and, just keep moving forward. Do not look back, unless it is to learn a lesson or find a positive. We can never walk in the past, its impossible. So, walk in the now.

Make your life your own. Design your perfect. Believe in you and all that you can accomplish with time, effort and some planning.

For some of you this will mean reinventing yourself, looking long and hard in the mirror at your past choices and experiences and asking yourself , 'am I where I am today because of fate, or because of the choices that I made?'

Some situations cannot be predicted or helped. You cannot control who your parents are, nor what your childhood is like. Yet as an adult you can chose to be the best parent you can be, despite your experiences.

Whatever our past, I know that we are more often than not where we are because of choices, those good or bad, spontaneous or planned, stupid or clever.

I want you to know that wherever you are, whatever your age, your situation that you can and will change things if you so desire.

The rest of your life is YOURS for the taking. It might seem like a long journey today, a steep hill, or even a mountainous landscape to traverse, but I promise you that when you get to your destination you can look back upon that journey with pride, knowing that you had the courage to put one foot in front of the other and get going.

As a survivor of childhood abuse I needed to write this book to show you that your past does not ever define your future. You can be whatever you want to be and that your tomorrow can be different from your today. Our futures are never written in tablets of stone on the day we are born.

As a child I counted down the years until I could leave the hell that I called home. I left at the earliest opportunity that I could. As a result, as an adult I refuse to accept unhappiness and relationships which do not bring me joy. I steer away from toxic relationships, falseness, jealousy, negativity and bitterness. I have no time in my world for them and no desire to be associated such people and emotions.

If you are reading this book, then I know that some of you may be seriously be thinking about change and what it may mean for you. It might be a tiny change, maybe to be more positive, or a huge life change, for instance changing a career, leaving a toxic relationship or addressing childhood trauma. What ever it is I know you can achieve it.

Of course, change is scary, uncomfortable and inevitably leads us on a different path to the one we're used to walking upon. But, ask yourself this, if you don't make the change, face the fear and move away from where you are now, what might you be missing out on? What beauty, success, environment, friendships and experiences might you be avoiding? What might life be like if you just go for it.

If you are comfortable where you are, and have just read this book because it was the first thing that you picked up, or you liked my front cover, that's cool. There's no pressure to change anything unless you want to, or unless you are ready. But, if you are a believer in fate, destiny and the LOA (Law Of Attraction) then, you might see this as a sign,

A, get off Your ass and change it because it sucks kind of sign,

A, you're not living, you're existing kind of sign,

A, someone else has had a tough few years, but has decided to change things for the better and I can do it too kind of sign.

Whatever your reason for picking up this book, please, please use it as it was intended.

Use it as that small, dark haired girl, born in the 70's with so many aspirations and hopes intended.

To inspire you to change, to be more than you thought you could be, and live a life that you design, by your rules.

Be brave, be tenacious and be positive.

I'll see you on the other side...............

16033055R00162

Printed in Great Britain
by Amazon